A Peach Tree
in an Apple Orchard

Tales of a Southerner's Life in Vermont

PAUL FERSEN

THE LYONS PRESS
Guilford, Connecticut
An imprint of The Globe
Pequot Press

The Lyons Press is an imprint of The Globe Pequot Press.

10 9 8 7 6 5 4 3 2 1

Printed in the United States of America

Designed by John Barnett/4 Eyes Design

ISBN 978-1-59921-152-7

Library of Congress Cataloging-in-Publication Data is available
on file.

To Grandma Moon

Contents

Foreword

The truly engaging writers—those we most look forward to reading—usually have a unique take on their material. We all live in the same world, after all, and what arrests us as readers is a new and unusual way of looking at it.

As the editor of *Stratton* magazine, the world I deal with is southwestern Vermont. This is the country of Robert Frost and Ethan Allen; a landscape of stone walls and sugar maples; a culture of old Yankee verities and customs. The *Stratton* contributor with the most . . . ah, *eccentric* take on this lovely, unique little piece of the globe is Paul Fersen, a Georgia native who starred for the University of Georgia football team (How 'bout them Dawgs!) and went on to play professionally for the New Orleans Saints, and then somehow made his way to Vermont. He is a big, gentle man who speaks with a molodic drawl that could not sound more alien here in the heart of New England.

But like a lot of us who came here from somewhere else, who *chose* Vermont and have been happy with the results, Paul loves this place. Loves it so much, in fact, that he embraced it at its most fundamental level. Paul got right down into the essence of Vermont and became a dairy farmer. For several years, he milked cows, spread manure, repaired fences and machinery and basically lived the life that so many of us like to romanticize but couldn't endure for a single day if we ever tried it.

Paul eventually left the farming game and took up office work. And while he was at it, he raised a family and wrote essays for *Stratton* magazine. He has always brought his unique view—a southern boy in New England—to everything he has written, that is to say, Bucko surveying his backyard (southern Vermont).

Like all of Paul's readers, I was charmed by his take on this part of the world and by the way things seem to happen to him. When he brought in the story of how he once left his dog in the front seat of his truck with the engine running . . . well, without reading, I *knew* what was going to happen next. Of course the dog—a Lab named Yoo Hoo (only Paul would name a dog after a revolting chocolate flavored drink that is popular in the south)—somehow managed to get the truck into gear, then drive off the driveway and into the woods. It was inevitable and funny . . . especially in Paul's telling.

Paul writes about the things that happen to him and the people who have been part of his life and the routine, daily events that in his telling become comic adventures.

We learn about—and come to love—"Grandma Moon." We laugh at Paul and his pals—and their dogs—hunting ducks in the Mettowee Valley. We appreciate dairy farming as almost an exercise in slapstick . . . the way Paul describes it, anyway.

Any magazine is lucky to land a writer who connects emotionally with its readership and who somehow keeps that connection going no matter what he writes about. I know from talking to readers of the magazine that Paul has made that connection. He has written many wonderful stories for *Stratton* and his loyal readers hope that there will be many more. His editor certainly shares this hope.

If you have never read Paul's stuff, then this book gives you an opportunity to be delighted. You can start anywhere. If, like me and the readers of *Stratton*, you are already a fan, you will no doubt find your favorite story here and find reason to smile again. I still don't know how he does it. He makes it look easy and that, as any writer will tell you, is the hardest thing to do.

MARSHA NORMAN
Editor, *Stratton* Magazine

Acknowledgments

I'd like to thank Marsha Norman and Lee Romano, respectively the editor and publisher of *Stratton* magazine, for encouraging me to create Bucko. Marsha had a clear vision of who Bucko was from the beginning. Lee gave me my first shot at using my journalism degree as editor of the magazine.

I'd like to thank Maureen Graney and The Lyons Press for letting me finally get all these stories in one place.

I'd like to thank my family, Mimi, Nicholas, Elizabeth and Cooper, who provided me with endless material over the past 20 years.

Finally I'd like to thank the southern culture and the Vermont culture for providing such marvelously fertile ground for humor.

Introduction

People who read my columns have often said I should write a book. I never paid much attention because knowing myself as I do, I didn't think I had the span of attention to write a book. When I write, I generally say what I need to say in about four to five typed pages and I'm done. Interestingly, if you do that long enough, lo and behold you have a book. Maybe there is hope.

For the past couple of decades, I've been writing a column for *Stratton* magazine, a lovely little ski resort magazine that is not so little anymore and has been around for over 40 years now. At one time in my early days here, I was the editor of this magazine, when it was a lot less interesting and attractive than it is now. I then graduated to columnist as I moved on to my next careers of farming and fishing.

I was born and raised in the south and was as indelibly marked with that culture as any man. I moved up here out of curiosity with no intention of staying, and find myself rooted in Vermont some 28 years later. The melding of these two cultures in one semi-irreverent human being proved to generate some unique observations of life, or so they tell me. These columns are the result.

If one has the perseverance to read this book, one will watch my children grow up, find out how different we are as a society from just a few years ago and how much the pace of life has increased even in this lovely backwater region. One of my early columns involved my consternation with computers, as did one of my most recent. The difference in the technology written 15 years apart is as different as the Paleozoic Era is from today. The world is changing faster than we realize, and going back and compiling these columns made that startlingly apparent. Living here in Vermont, it is easy to lose track of the ever-accelerating pace of life until you suddenly look back in earnest.

Writing this book was enjoyable, mainly because I didn't realize I was writing a book. It is intended to entertain one chapter at a time, just as I wrote it one chapter at a time. It covers dogs, children, farming, parenthood, country living, trucks, hunting, fishing and life in general. The social commentary in these columns was never intended to alter behavior patterns, only to make you smile and occasionally laugh at the often ridiculous things we do as we go about our lives. Perhaps in some of these columns you might suddenly see yourself and realize how humorous life can be if we just step back and strip away our pretense and pride. Life can be pretty funny if you just let it.

Hunting and Fishing

The Pawlet Duck and Retriever Club

Migrating ducks travel along "flyways" that follow large bodies of water lying in a north-south path. Among them are the heavily traveled interstates of the waterfowl universe, like the Atlantic coast flyway and the Mississippi flyway. Lesser flyways such as the Champlain-Hudson and the Connecticut River feed into these majors. And then . . . there is the Mettowee Valley flyway, the two-lane blacktop of the duck world. If it were a highway, it would be lined with small motels with individual cabins; souvenir stands selling moccasins and maple syrup or, further south, boiled peanuts and stuffed baby gators. It might be the path taken by ducks looking to discover the charms of the heartland.

There are two schools of thought as to the intelligence of the ducks that take this path. One has it that this is the intelligent duck route, which they take to avoid the high traffic and heavily hunted routes such as the Atlantic flyway where they would run a veritable gauntlet of gunfire. The contrary opinion is that these ducks are merely stupid and lost. Whatever the case, it is demonstrably true that there aren't very many ducks—smart or stupid—flying along the Mettowee.

Still, in the late days of autumn, these feathered few encounter the Pawlet Duck and Retriever Club. A small (very small) group of overly optimistic duck hunters for whom the fact that you might even see a duck is reason enough to climb out of bed on a frozen November morning and go sit on the bank of a river to watch the sun come up.

There are only six of us, give or take the occasional guest—myself, Murph, Tom, and the three dogs (this means that one of the dogs has to hold office under the normal President, Vice-President, Secretary, Treasurer hierarchy), but this where we live and this is what we love.

Our clubhouse is Tom's place, located directly on the shores of the Mettowee. Nearly every morning of the duck season we gather here before work at around 5:00 a.m. for coffee. Tramping into Tom's kitchen in waders and boots, we stand in one area to avoid tracking mud and debris into the rest of the house and keep ourselves in the good graces of Tom's lovely and extremely tolerant wife. The dogs meet and greet with raised hackles and noses shoved in disgusting places until they discover they're best friends. Then, they proceed to race relentlessly through the house in search of bones and toys. Our cars are loaded with decoys, hunting stools, kennels and guns. Were one to do a per-duck expense report, each duck harvested would be worth a small engagement ring. There is, however, one compensating economic advantage to hunting ducks in southern Vermont—you don't spend much on ammunition.

We members of the PDRC work together at Orvis, which allows us a bit of leeway to pursue the elusive duck, as it is, in fact, part of our business. Essentially we hunt two areas. On mornings when duty calls and we need to make an early meeting, we simply walk down the hill from Tom's deck, put our decoys in the river and kick back in the bushes. I think we actually shot three ducks here last season, but the coffee was good and the conversation better.

On those mornings when time permits, we head for the "Lease," a secret section of the river, kept private by the fact that nobody else gives a damn. Here the river opens up and when the ducks see this big stretch of water and its slow, wide pools, they frequently set their wings and drop. When the weather gets cold and the still waters of the valley freeze over, these pools suddenly become attractive for their open water.

On the walk in to the "Lease," we are accompanied by the trio of Labradors—a frenzied, whirling dance troupe of otter tails and enthusiasm. Once out of the car, they scream across the pastures in pursuit of nothing but freedom. Flo is the matriarchal ten-year-old who belongs to Murph. She has seen ducks on the major West Coast flyways and her heroic retrieves are legion.

Trilly is Tom's driven adolescent whose decoy retrieves far outnumber her duck retrieves. This could be our fault—she has seen far more decoys than actual dead ducks—and, anyway, her desire and willingness to hurl herself into freezing rivers is legendary and her focus on the sky and its denizens is truly uncanny. Trilly is also famous for her games of keep-away, and is often seen headed upriver, duck (or decoy) in mouth with Tom in hot pursuit, screaming NO! Perhaps the ultimate dog/ owner moment came when Tom literally dove through the air to tackle his dog and the two wrestled in the mud like bimbos in a beer commercial.

My dog Pickett is the infant, a young chocolate who made his first appearance in the blind at four months and promptly curled up on a decoy bag and went to sleep. As the season progressed and he grew stronger, he watched Flo and Trilly until one day toward the end of the season, he strained at the lead imploring me to let him have his turn. Flo had led Trilly into the water as a pup and imbued her with her incredible desire to retrieve. Trilly did the same for Pickett. His first tentative steps in the water are now Herculean leaps thanks to Trilly's example. To watch them together crashing headlong into the current is a retriever owner's great joy.

When we hunt the "Lease," we put out the decoys and then spread out in the hedgerow to wait. We separate partially to cover more of the river, but more importantly to keep the dogs separated and quiet. This is generally fruitless as all three love to warn us of approaching ducks (or duck as it were) by barking as loudly as possible.

Murph is the veteran duck hunter and, as such, the resident caller. When he cuts loose with a hail call or feeding chuckle, the ducks generally turn and take a look. However, Murph is a bit hard of hearing so between the dogs barking and us screaming at him to call, we generally scare away the few lost souls that do happen by our hunting ground. Tom's shotgun is legendary for jamming at just the right moment. I remember wondering once, when ducks were actually coming in, why he wasn't shooting. When I looked over, I saw him banging his shotgun against a fence post.

In truth, there were some great days on the Mettowee, "great" being a relative term. There are, in fact, no "bad" days duck hunting, only unsuccessful ones. Most of the time we walk out of the field with a bag full of decoys and some disappointed dogs, but every once in a while we get lucky and take a limit. Later in the morning, the office will be regaled with stories of incredible shots and heroic retrieves.

I remember an e-mail from one of our colleagues recounting a trip to Stuttgart, Arkansas—duck hunting capital of the world—where he and his guides saw thousands of ducks and had their limit in minutes. I think this would be intriguing once or twice—to say I'd done it and just to see that many ducks. But I don't think I would trade my valley in Vermont and my hunting companions for any of it. I've huddled by the river, hands wrapped around a warm cup, and watched a cloud paint a mountainside with ice. I've witnessed blood red skies and fields, touched by the first sunlight, suddenly shimmer as if covered with scattered diamonds. I've shared time and laughter with two great friends and three remarkable dogs. The few duck breasts I have savored over the course of the year and the memories of each successful hunt are vivid in their rarity. Stuttgart may be a great place to hunt, but it depends on what you're hunting. Me? I'm hunting more than just ducks.

Transvestites in the Spring Woods

Easy there. Don't get your camo underwear in a bunch. I realize this is a racy theme for this staid publication, but we're talking turkey hunting here, that ritual of spring where a bunch of guys in camo sit around in the woods doing their best to imitate female turkeys in order to entice randy male turkeys into range. It's Vermont's version of *La Cage Aux Folles*. Once in range and just as the turkey thinks he's going to get lucky, we nail 'em. (Oddly familiar, somehow.)

Of course this doesn't mean we dress up like a female turkey. Instead we dress up like trees and bushes so we can sit motionless for hours, blending into the landscape and lying in wait for our wary prey. And let me assure you, they are wary. Turkeys can't smell very well and they can't hear all that well, but their vision is one of the wonders of nature. "Eyes in the back of his head" is not a misnomer with Thomas, as he can see 300 degrees without moving his head and his vision is monocular as opposed to binocular, which means he sees everything in one shot without having to move. Basically the wild turkey is an IMAX theater with wings.

There are probably those of you out there that think hunting turkeys is cruel and inhuman. You're right, but generally for the hunter, not the huntee. As evidence of this, turkeys routinely baffle, stupefy and downright embarrass the hunter, and I for one rank as one of the top baffled, stupefied and embarrassed hunters in the valley. Fortunately I'm not alone and for every hunter that fools ol' Tom there are more than a few that don't.

When calling in a turkey, the hunter locates a gobbler by listening for his distinctive and spectacular gobbles. It's truly one of the magnificent sounds of the spring woods and will turn the most seasoned hunter into a quivering mass of uncertainty. When gobbling, the turkey is essentially telling the women in his life where he is and that he's ready for some action. He accentuates this vocal behavior by going into full display to show off what a tough guy he is. (Remarkably similar in attitude to the adolescent human male at spring break who leaps off the third story hotel balcony into the pool, but I never did that.)

When in display the turkey spreads his feathers into a huge fan and puffs out his chest just like all the pictures we've seen since childhood. This is the only time they do this, folks. Any other time of the year, they look just like any other turkey. It occurred to me once as I sat listening in the woods, all those Thanksgiving cards and posters I made for my Mom where I traced my hand to make a turkey, all the decorations on my grammar school bulletin board, and the little turkey candles that graced my Grandma's Thanksgiving table were a bunch of oversexed gobblers looking for a good time. God help us if Jerry Falwell ever figures this out.

Once a gobbler is located, the hunter finds a spot, sets up and begins to do his best to sweet-talk the gobbler into coming within range. The hunter does this by imitating hen yelps and purrs with a variety of instruments designed to make these sounds. Basically it's phone sex in a weird language using instruments such as mouth diaphragms, call boxes, pieces of slate with strikers or anything else that will make a sound not unlike running your fingernails over a blackboard.

There is one particular bird that I hunt every year and every year he conjures up some diabolical scheme to make me look like an idiot. What's diabolical about it is that each time he maneuvers me to failure, he makes sure that when I discover my mistake, he's watching and that I know it. Each year as I step into the abyss of stupidity, I look up to see him standing there with a big gobbler grin on his face for the split second before he lifts off, not to be seen or heard until the next year.

This past year we conversed for more than an hour, him shaking the trees with his ebullient gobbles and me doing my best *Meleagris gallopavo silvestris* version of Mae West to entice him into my leafy boudoir. Eventually he went silent and I heard nothing from him (the cad) for about 20 minutes. I was not going to make the "mistake" again this year so I sat silently with my gun in position, scanning the woods for the slightest movement—the black widow waiting for her prey. (This pretending to be a female is weird). Anyway, I heard nothing (just like a man). Finally, I couldn't stand it a moment longer. I slooowly reached down to my left to pick up my box call to give him one last irrefutable reason to rendezvous. I heard a slight rustle and raised my eyes. There, not 20 yards away, stood the bird, staring at me with what seemed an expression of both amusement and sympathy for the stupid human. With that he lifted off and headed down the valley like a B-2 bomber, wings set in beautiful flight and for the rest of the year, totally undetectable.

In truth if it were about the killing, I would have quit long ago as my hunting techniques are basically making the world safe for turkeys. If I am lucky enough to harvest one and enjoy the occasional smoked breast, all the better, but what really makes this worthwhile is listening to Vermont wake up from its winter slumber. Perhaps no outdoor experience is ironically quite as peaceful as hunting in the Vermont spring woods at first light and listening to the natural progression of waking creatures. Eerily silent in darkness, the forest gently lightens, cueing the first notes of songbirds, followed soon by the staccato peal of the pileated woodpeckers. The crow choir joins the chorus a few moments later and amid this accompaniment, the gobbler rings forth with his solo to let the world and his harem know that he is alive and well. It is so consistent, so orchestrated, and yet each morning there is some subtle variation on the theme. That's the reason I go out there and for me it's the best thing I do, even if I have to act like a girl to do it.

Coop's Fish

Every little boy has a fish out there. And a friend, too.

At times he seems like a father, though only a few years older than me. Perhaps it's his knowledge, at least when it comes to fish and the ocean. I always feel like a child next to him, learning—more importantly wanting to please. It's been that way since that first night on a black and squally Atlantic beach where he seemed so sure and comfortable and me so disoriented, trying to cast in the dark.

When it comes to the business we share, the roles reverse and I look on him as someone to protect as I would my own. As confident as he is on the water, in business he's naïve—honest to a fault. A rare man indeed. Which is why my youngest bears his name: Cooper.

The pilgrimage to his island comes with inherent freedoms. When the ferry leaves the dock, the bonds of accountability begin to fray. Once ensconced in the beach house, rods and waders scattered along the porch rail, the release is complete. Beyond the Elizabeth Islands the mainland remains at bay, unable to burden me with the grinding weight of responsibility.

This year was different. Coop's heart was struggling. Too many years of blue-collar cuisine. The smile and the warmth were there as always, and little Coop didn't notice the gray pallor where sun-burnished leather once glowed. He only knew those thick and weathered arms that encircled him loved him and were taking him fishing.

I noticed. He shrugged as if it were nothing, but the worry in Lela's and Tina's eyes spoke volumes. I talked with them quietly while Coop took the boy to see the eel tank.

"Apparently there's a significant blockage," Lela said, moving quickly around the room. Stopping too long allowed too much time to think, to let the worst creep in. Tina watched her mother and then looked at me with the flicker of a smile.

"We're so glad you're here," she said, wrapping her arms around my waist and burying her head in my chest. As though I could somehow solve this problem as I had solved a few minor business problems for them in the past.

The house is up-island near Gay Head, a small cluster of houses gathered together overlooking Lobsterville Beach, the nearest resemblance of a store some five miles distant. Even on the busiest weekends this long stretch of beach remains unpopulated, the tourists concentrated down-island where the ferries land. Somehow some dim tribal instinct offers comfort in numbers, and they seem content with what they can find close by. Thank God for my genetic deficiency.

Lobsterville is a fishing beach, stretching from Menemsha Pond up to the cliffs of Gay Head. Across the sound, the Elizabeth Islands stretch westward. The bloody sunsets over Cutty Hunk are familiar to anglers just stepping on the beach for a night's fishing, and in June the stripers gather here fresh from their northward migration, covered in seal lice and voracious. Menemsha Pond spews billions of sand eel fry with the outgoing tide, and the striped bass feast here for weeks. At night as the tide sweeps the eels west along the beach, the big fish hang by the conveyor gulping big holes in the dark sea.

The house is perfectly situated overlooking a huge stretch of beach, and we could watch the birds and the bait without leaving the deck. In the evenings as the sea darkens and the sky goes blood red, we watch the surf line for swirls and the nervous water of trembling baitfish. This year we were treated to a phenomenon we'd never seen: a nightly fluke blitz. Normally fluke are content to lie in wait, darting up to snatch their prey while posing as the bottom. For some reason Mother Nature had encouraged them to become school feeders and attack this line of sand eels in the Lobsterville surf.

Looking down the beach, we saw the water churning with small swirls and flat fluke popping up in the air like pancakes on a diner griddle. Little Cooper was beside himself wanting to catch some fish.

Big Coop wasn't allowed to fish—doctor's orders—and Tina and Lela were as solid as the rocks at Devil's Bridge in refusing to let him sneak out for few hours. But little Coop's arrival brought a softening and a "maybe" when he begged to go fishing.

"Just for an hour."

"No more."

"We'll be down at sunset," Coop said, as he began searching through the turmoil of his garage for a little rod for the four-year-old. I watched him for a few moments and smiled, thinking he was as purposeful for this small expedition as he would be preparing for an offshore tuna trip.

"You're sure this is all right?" I questioned Lela.

"This is the only exception I'd make," she said. "Fishing with Coopie will do him more good than anything I can think of. But only for a bit. Tina and I will both be there to make sure he doesn't overdo it." Together we watched him rig the little rod.

We were all on the beach that evening—Joey, Matt and me outfitted like an assault team: waders, chest packs, fly rods, wading jackets. Everyone else—Coop, Lela, Tina, little Coop, Mimi and Lizzie—were dressed lightly as they would leave the beach when the sun dipped behind the islands.

Coop rigged the rod with a white Slug-Go and a bobber. He flipped the rig into the sea, set the drag and handed the rod to my little boy standing by his side in bare feet and an oversized sweatshirt, trembling and ex-pectant in the night air.

For nearly an hour the child laughed at the tug of fluke as he and Coop moved back and forth with the surf, big Coop casting and removing fish, little Coop reeling and squealing with delight as each fluke appeared in the wash. The little rod doubled over with the slightest tug, and for the boy, each fish was an epic struggle.

The striper hit just as the sun dropped below Cutty Hunk. Crimson streaks were racing across the sky when we noticed a change in little Coop—just enough of an inflection in timbre to nudge squeals of joy toward help-lessness. The line was peeling off the reel, and it was obvious this was no fluke. I grabbed him as he stumbled toward the water reeling furiously, his little hands trying to keep up. The spool began to reveal itself and suddenly the knot appeared. I held on to little Coop and waited for the inevitable sound of snapping mono. But the fish stopped.

Little Coop was in a four-year-old frenzy, trying to reel against the big fish. He was getting nowhere, the drag on the tiny spinning reel allowing no gain. Big Coop kneeled next to him and gently held him around the waist. I stepped away. He began to whisper to the boy. Immediately he calmed and began reeling while the rod bent toward the sand.

"Christ, Coop. How much line is on that thing?"

Coop looked at me with a grin.

"Twenty-five yards of six-pound."

"No way." I fish striper with 200 yards of backing and 16-pound tippet. My son was fighting this fish with a horseshoe's toss of six-pound test.

For 20 minutes we stood transfixed by the struggle between big fish and small boy. Although he was my son, I stepped back and left him in the hands of Coop, kneeling there, the little boy wrapped tightly in his arms and reeling, reeling, constantly reeling while Coop whispered encouragement. There could be no better way for my son to catch his first striper.

At a certain point the battle seemed to be too much for the boy and the tears welled up in his eyes. His tiny arms were failing and the fish seemed no closer now than before. He kept looking at Coop, who tightened his grip and whispered something again, calming him immediately. On occasion the two Coops gained, but always the big striper then moved easily away, stripping line from the tiny reel but always, as the spool knot appeared, stopping, turning, and allowing the boy to pull her back toward the beach. Salty tracks glistened on more than a few cheeks as we who loved these two Coops watched our old friend and his namesake do exactly what nature intended: catch a great fish together.

The fourth time the fish came to heel, she stayed. Coop gently pulled the boy back up the beach and slid the fish across the sand until it was clear of the wash. Cheers erupted, cameras flashed and Coop reached for the fish. Little Coop's eyes widened as a three-foot striped bass lay staring at him, its gills moving heavily. Coop pulled the fish up and held it for the little boy, urging him to get closer for a picture. The sheer size of the striper frightened little Coop, but he stepped closer, reaching out to Coop for reassurance while eyeing the fish warily.

The cameras flashed again, and I took the fish from Coop and walked out into the surf to release her. As she began to move I held only her tail, waiting for that powerful shake that would assure me of her revival. I looked at her curiously. She could have snapped that line with one halfhearted shake of her head, but she didn't. Her tail easily could have propelled her out of danger, but it didn't. I pulled her back one more time. She looked at me with her bottomless black eye, shook her tail and moved off into the dark water.

Perhaps every little boy has a fish out there. I hope that's the order of things. My son was fortunate to meet his—even more so wrapped in the arms of one who loved both him and the fish so much. Ever so rarely, fate offers up a moment of such perfection that one struggles later to relate it without crushing sentimentality. I grinned to myself as I walked slowly back toward the beach. This one will be the hardest tale to tell.

The Swamp Haint

He owns this swamp. Ain't no doubt about that, his morning roll call moving the moss like a hot August zephyr. He's tucked himself into 3,000 acres of hardwood ridges tumbling into river-bottom swamps in an oxbow of the Alabama River. Not but one way to get in and out of his kingdom less you want a pre-dawn swim in the Alabama.

It's the finest turkey ground I've ever seen. These ridges have never been logged. Thick, old hardwoods shade the open floor. I've been in a few cathedrals. I've been in these woods a few times. The similarity ain't lost on me. Both places are quiet, the kind of quiet that instills reverence in even the most feckless heathen. In one you hear footsteps on marble as clear as the tapping of a woodpecker in the other. Both of 'em confirm your insignificance.

These ridges come in through the neck of the oxbow and drop steeply into the palmetto bottoms. There's ravines that could swallow buildings and a misstep in the dark morning would be your end. The top branches of the biggest of these old bucks, rooted in the bottom of the ravines, don't even reach the top edge.

Where the ridges die out, the bottoms begin. The bottoms are swept and purged every year by thick, reddish Alabama water. What's left is a dark forest of old bearded oaks and cypress reaching out over dunes and sloughs cut and carved by the old sculptress. That she is old is evidenced by the sand dollars embedded high in her bluffs some 100 miles from the nearest salt water. Cypress swamps and palmetto thickets push endlessly under the canopy offering a thousand hog wallers, deer beds and turkey roosts. This is the kingdom of the Swamp Haint, the biggest bird I've ever seen, with prehistoric tracks and a beard of Gandalfian proportions.

This land once belonged to Red Eagle, though true to his culture he would never claim ownership of the land. That is a peculiarity of the white man. He was perhaps better known as William Weatherford, half-breed chief of the Creeks, son of an English-speaking trapper who married a great-granddaughter of the first Sehoy, Princess of the Wind Clan. He led the bloodiest Indian massacre on American soil at Ft. Mims on the confluence of the Alabama and Tombigbee rivers, fought Jackson at Horseshoe Bend, was captured and ultimately pardoned for his great bravery. He spent the rest of his life on this ground.

Not much has changed here since then. Only the dark creosote hunting camp, tucked in the far reach of the oxbow, suggests a difference. Once a year, Jimbo and I retreat here to elude the twenty-first century and to hunt turkeys—big turkeys, in particular the Swamp Haint. Jimbo saw him first.

We'd come in from the morning's hunt. At dawn the air is crisp and the senses are sharpened by the cold. By late morning, the hot sun and six hours of hunting have relegated us to the front porch for shade, coffee and chewing tobacco. I'd been up on Jasey's field hunting birds in the big hardwoods. Jimbo had been in the swamp. He sat there tinkering with a slate call looking for the sweet spot. The air hummed with the sound of the bees that nested in the porch roof, their switch suddenly flipped by the sun's heat. They were huge bees that raced around bumping into each other and flying right up to your face where they would hover in some kind of bizarre staring contest. Slater Hanks called 'em "study bees," "'cause they come up and study ya."

"He was as big as I've ever seen. Big ol' beard draggin' the ground. He was up on a big dune on the other side of a slough. I called and he strutted and stomped and drummed and spit for an hour, but he just wouldn't come over the slough. Man he was somthin'."

"How far?"

"'Bout 40 yards, but I wasn't gonna chance that shot with a 20 gauge."

Jimbo's not into firepower. Hunting skill is the attraction, the killing secondary. He hunts ducks to great success with a 20.

"No chance to move?"

"No cover, nowhere to go. I was sitting behind one scrawny palmetto. Man he was big. How 'bout you?"

"Tar baby he don't say nothin'." Code words for a silent morning. "You gonna try and roost him tonight?" After dinner we'd go out and roost birds before coming back for a last cup of coffee and a chew before bed. We'd sit on the porch listening to the night and every so often flick on the big handheld spotlight. Inevitably a dozen pairs of devil eyes would peer back from the treeline.

"Nope."

"How come?"

"You are."

Jimbo is nothing if not generous. He'd had his chance at the Haint and now he wanted me to have mine. I protested, knowing full well Jimbo would never recant. He never does on matters of principle. Offering a friend a shot at a trophy gobbler was a matter of pure principle.

Jimbo's taillights disappeared in the field and I stood on the path into the river bottoms. The southern sun was flickering through the palmetto leaves like green shutters in a low country courtyard. I moved quickly down the road, wanting to get to the strut ground so I could check out positions for the morning hunt. I found the dune and the tracks—big tracks—T. rex tracks. Jimbo was right. This was one big-ass bird. I snapped off a few palmetto fans, sat down under a tree on the end of the dune and stuck the fans in front of me. I was there to roost him, but if he showed himself in the right place I had no compunctions about ambush.

The bugs came in a fury. Gnats and mosquitos flew right through the DEET, biting through my sleeves, banging into my eyes. I decided to practice my Zen meditation to ignore the itch and aggravation. It soon occurred to me there are no gnats in Nepal. I reverted to my southern heritage, simply grittin' my teeth, cussin' and trying not to move.

A hen came in from behind and landed in my tree. I learned more about cackling and purring than all the Knight and Hale tapes could ever offer, but I was pinned. A few minutes later, I heard the Haint. The wingbeats recalled Grandma Moon whacking carpets with a broom, limbs cracked and men trembled as the Haint found his way up to his perch. Once seated, he thrust his head skyward and poured forth a Brobdingnagian gobble that shook the swamp and informed its denizens that he was home for the night.

For two hours I sat motionless, joints seizing like a junkyard motor. By the time it was dark enough to belly crawl into the slough and away from the roosted birds, the pain from old age and new bites was agonizing. Great things come only from great sacrifice and this bastard was mine.

Light river sand in the grass track was my GPS back to the edge of the swamp. It would be my guide in the black of the morning. I could feel the truck before I reached it.

"Find him?" Jimbo's question emanated from the darkness.

"Damn straight. He's everything you said."

"You gonna get him?"

Turkey wisdom and superstition bid caution here, but I succumbed.

"I got him locked in."

Even though I couldn't see Jimbo, I knew he was grinnin'.

The trail turned to pure river sand and even in the blackness, I knew the slough was in front of me, and the dune to my right. I eased into the slough, reaching out to the right to feel the side of the dune, keeping it between me and the Haint. I reached the end of the dune where it dropped off into the palmetto flats. I crawled up in the mercifully quiet sand and set up. The plateau of the dune spread before me and yesterday's strut zone was now a kill zone.

Straight up five brought forth a booming reveille. Then another—another. Full-throated gobbles rocked the surrounding woods as the Haint called to his harem. I offered one three-note tree yelp that was cut off with a heavy-handed response. I waited for two minutes and then clucked twice. That was it. No way was I blowing this. I slid the mouth call into my cheek and let it sit like a wad of good Carolina leaf.

For an hour the Haint rang forth. Hunched under my tree like Quasimoto in the bell tower, I knew he was coming. Each thunderous pronouncement broadened my smile. He was mine. Wingbeats brought my gun into position covering the zone.

The gobble changed—fainter? 'Cause he's on the ground? The next, even less. He was walking away.

Damn! I thrust the mouth call back in the roof of my mouth and pleaded my case like a starving hooker. The last gobble was contemptuous, the swamp silent. My final entreaty answered only by the gnats.

Jimbo was leaning on the bumper spittin' juice on the ground when I stepped into the field. He saw the empty hands and offered a smile of shared experience.

"Dya see him?"

"Yep."

"Smart, ain't he?"

I grinned back and reached for my own tobacco. We leaned against the truck and listened to the swamp.

* * *

Epilogue

Jimbo's nephew Bill, a noted turkey hunter in his own right, went down two weeks later to hunt the Haint. From what I understand he got even closer than me, but the Haint treated him with the same merciless contempt.

Say what you please, I take solace in my belief that the tormented chief of the Creeks, William Weatherford, stills walks this ground—now the tormentor.

Full Circle

I remember the heat. Not the weighted air that drove gallused old men to shade, but the sweet heat of shirt-less barefoot boys in the south Georgia sun—though the two are one and the same. Grandma Moon didn't go fishing less'n it was hot, the day's sunrise finding the mules already ensconced under the nearest pasture oak. She settled for a two-acre straw hat, an old cotton dress with apron, and wore-out orthopedic shoes; the kind all southern spinster teachers wore, 'cept theirs didn't have the holes in 'em. She wore this near every day I remember, as her brand of fishing didn't require much in the way of technical apparel.

Lula Virginia Henrietta Belle Woolfolk Moon was a meat fisherman. She wouldn't mind the term fisherman since Grandma was no feminist. There isn't a feminist in the world could survive her day, much less her life. She cooked, cleaned, buried a child, fought forest fires, killed rattlers and guided her family through the Depression, paying college tuitions with barrels of soup mix she made. That's what you did then. She opened her house to the young boys from Benning to give them a piece of her home before they died in places like Bastogne and the Hurtgen Forest.

She arrived on the farm in 1912 in the back of Grand-daddy Moon's wagon and lived there until the twentieth century surrounded and swallowed the farm. It broke her heart—and mine. There were 2,000 acres when she got there. The old house stood on piers to keep it cool in the summer and provide shade and comfort underneath to the assorted hounds of questionable lineage whose only task was to keep the henhouse fox free and the garden safe from pillaging rabbits. I'm not sure they knew this was their job, but simply achieved success by their mere presence. It was enough to grant them sanctuary and sustenance in a world where that was more privilege than practice.

The kitchen was separate from the house to keep it from burning down. Massive oak and pecan trees, the largest of which was the biggest tree in the county when Grandma arrived, surrounded the house. That pecan tree witnessed the building of the house long before the war. Yankee cavalry rested in its shade, and this little boy claimed its branches as his own private domain. The rest of the place was pine woods and pecan orchards, a barefoot boy's dream. There were two ponds on the place and these were the protein mines from which Grandma dredged the shiny, flopping prize that, along with chickens, hogs and a garden the size of Muscogee County, kept her family alive and well during the harshest period of the twentieth century. The chickens and hogs weren't much fun and a garden that size is numbing, but fishing was pure pleasure for a woman who had no time for such things.

"Go get the worms, punkin." Some of the first words I remember. Early on I learned to go out back to the massive rusted washtub that was her bait factory, resting in the shade of the big oak. I'd reach down deep into the cool mixture of dried manure, coffee grounds, black earth and wood shavings and pull out a huge handful of nightcrawlers and garden worms, stuff them in an old Nescafe can poked full of holes and run back to where she was preparing for the afternoon's harvest. I didn't have to wash my hands neither. "Dirt's good for a child. That's all we are anyways."

The cane poles leaned in the corner where the tin porch roof slid under the weathered clapboards. Grandma grabbed all eight in one heap of burnished cane, red and white floats of various size and dimension, and line.

Line everywhere. She dropped them into the two mule shoes welded to the top of her '51 Plymouth.

It has always been my contention she invented the first car-top rod rack. She got tired of trying to drive down to the pasture or out to Peed's Lake with eight 15-foot poles poking out the window, the butt ends jammed down into the floorboards, so she invented a rod rack. She went down to one of the sharecroppers who still lived on the farm and was a blacksmith by trade. We still had a draft mule or two on the farm back then. She had him weld a couple of big mule shoes to the Plymouth just above the doors. She could drop all eight cane poles in those shoes, tie them down with baling twine and drive unencumbered to the fishing hole, her grandbaby tucked next to her with his feet just dangling over the edge of those massive seats, or even sometimes standing so I could see where we were going. My seatbelt was Grandma Moon's right arm, which moved in tandem with her right foot when it hit the brake, pushing me back into the seat.

The pond was no more than a good acre, but it was deep and a few big trees offered shade near the bank. Grandma would have no part of the shade. She needed the space to kill fish. She spread the rods along the bank, and walking to each one systematically baited the hook, varying the height of the bobbers to find the right depth, spit on the worm and flipped it out into the pond. She'd light up a cigarette and patrol those rods with a hawk's eye searching the tiny red buoys for the slightest hint of a ripple. The instant a bobber disappeared, the fish would find itself transported from its dark, cool domain to green grass and sunshine in the time it takes to spit on bait. A piece of baling twine with a stick tied to both ends served as Miz Moon's cooler. One stick stuck in the ground and the other stick was passed longways through the gills and then turned sideways to hold the fish on the stringer. It wasn't long before 20 or more bream, and an occasional bass, lay in the shallow water "suckin' twine."

Miz Moon only owned one purse. It was a huge black patent leather affair all southern ladies carried. It went with her to church, Bible class, to Daughters of the American Revolution and Daughters of the Confederacy meetings. It was also her tackle box. In that cavernous bag lay lace handkerchiefs, an old wallet too full of life's memories to close, a change purse, tins of split shot, bobbers, a big pocket knife, gun oil, leaking jars of Uncle Josh's pork rinds, perfume, pliers, snelled hooks and the ever-present bottle of turpentine, which she used to soothe her arthritis.

Sitting in church with her on Sunday, the pulpit thundered with good southern damnation and salvation and I wandered through Grandma's purse and all its wonders waiting for the invitational hymn, "Just As I Am," which always signaled the beginning of the end. Reverend Walker, red-faced and sweating from his exhortations, would make us sing it over and over until at least three souls were saved. As there were less than a hundred people in the congregation we sometimes sang that hymn for what seemed hours to this little boy. Fortunately there were those in the flock that seemed to need salvation once a week, but all I knew was God's work was cutting into my fishin' time with Grandma.

The cane pole passed from my experience 40 years ago. My closets are full of graphite and machined aluminum and the fly boxes and tackle boxes are brimming with spectacular offerings to fool and cajole fish. There are times when the sheer volume of the equipment exasperates and decisions must be made—the right or wrong of it sucking the pleasure out of the experience—a far cry from the simple act of picking up a cane pole and a can of worms. Life is hindered now by the numbing weight of possessions and responsibilities each requiring decision. I stand naked and accessible to the world through e-mails, voicemails, cell phones and ever-accelerating levels of expectation. The torrent of decision tumbles endlessly like waves on the rocks and desperately, more and more, I find myself searching for silence.

This past spring I went to Alabama to hunt turkeys with Jimbo, a good friend and another southern boy raised on cane poles and bream. On a sultry afternoon after a morning hunt we decided to fish the farm ponds for dinner. Both Jimbo and I carry thousands of dollars of fishing tackle in our trucks, but it was by chance we passed an old country store. We stopped to get coffee and some chewing tobacco and there in the front was a box with ten 15-foot cane poles, rigged and ready for fishing for $5. For $12 I got a fully rigged pole, 50 crickets, a bag of pork cracklings and a pack of good Carolina leaf chewing tobacco. Life perceptibly slowed in that moment and memories of Miz Moon and the old Weems Road store, with the rusty tin roof and the faded Royal Crown Cola ads painted on the clapboards, flickered and darted into the light from where buried for years.

An hour later I stood on the bow of the old john boat in overalls and T-shirt holding a long burnished cane pole, flipping the bobber out under the overhangs into the chocolate water, hauling in bull bream. By dinner we had a Moon-sized stringer of golden fish and I had momentarily found silence. I was a boy again, yet unencumbered. I watched that pole bend to the water and felt the tug I had so long forgotten for there is no tug quite like the simple bend of southern bamboo.

My children love to fish, but the little one is the one blessed by the angling spirits. There are those chosen few among anglers who are truly gifted with the touch. These piscatorial pied pipers have some spiritual connection that reaches into the depths and connects with our finned brethren. I've known hundreds of anglers, but only a handful carry that gene, the gene that pulls fish from the depths while those around watch their offerings drift aimlessly. Grandma Moon was one, my little boy Coop is another. He's named after a great fisherman; he's caught more big fish than any child has a right to. I need not set the alarm in the morning to go fishing as he will be standing by my bedside at 4:00 a.m. inexplicably awakened. While I often struggle to rise, it is as if the fish call him in the early hours and say, "it's time." He is his great-grandmother incarnate.

It occurred to me in that john boat in Alabama, I had inadvertently denied my boy fishing in its purest form, pulling slab-sided bluegills from the depths with a stick and a string. He had learned his craft from infancy with his father's weapons and though he didn't know the difference, it became startlingly clear to me it was an injustice needing rectification.

I presented the pole to him this summer at the cabin, just as the sun was dropping through the trees. The varnished cane wrapped with line and bobber glistened in the twilight. He took the pole and, unwrapping the line, seemed to know exactly what to do. Baiting the hook and spitting on the bait as I taught him, he flipped the bobber and hook out into the dark water and stood motionless, staring at the little red ball. In an instant he pulled up and the rod tip shot to the water, the bobber skimming across the surface as the big bluegill turned its side to him and fought furiously. The arc of the long pole magnified the pull and his eyes widened in delight.

"Daddy!! It's a whopper!"

I stepped back for he didn't need me now. I watched him for the next hour as dusk turned to dark, hauling his flopping prey to the dock, the little barefoot boy with cane pole in hand, reaching into the water and into my heart. Perhaps in no other moment have I ever seen myself as clearly in my children. I was in fact, watching myself. Somewhere Miz Moon was spittin' on her bait and smiling and it occurred to me, in a world accelerating far too much for my liking, there are brief moments when I can find peace. Watching my barefoot boy with his cane pole is certainly one.

Lobsterville

"Christ, this looks like a war zone," I said quietly to my partner. We were sitting in the sand near midnight. The big chopper moved slowly along the beach, its twin halogen searchlights turning blackness into patches of brilliant daylight. Up and down the beach small groups of fishermen were silhouetted briefly, trudging up and down the beach in twos and threes, looking more like SEAL assault teams caught under flares than tournament anglers. In that light, with thumping chopper blades pounding your ears, chest packs and fly rods suddenly take on the look of combat gear.

"They must be looking for that kid," he said. Earlier some "civilians" canvassed the beach asking all the fly rodders if they'd seen a boy in a canoe over the past few hours. They had no gear, only street shoes and concern. None had seen the boy.

My partner and I were strangers. That's how the Vineyard Catch and Release tournament works. You fill out your application and they choose partners to fish together to verify each other's catches since all fish are released. It's not a high-profile tournament; it's just an excuse to go fishing. That's what a tournament is, a brilliantly contrived excuse to go fishing

"Honey, this is not just a fishing trip, it's an important tournament." That point alone serves to substantially reduce the guilt factor in my mind, which functions well using twisted, self-serving rationalization when it comes to fishing. This will not be fun; this is business—as if this is going to eliminate our mortgage. She acquiesces as usual with the knowing smile that tacitly acknowledges I'm full of shit. It's why I married her.

Say what you will, it takes me to Martha's Vineyard for a week's fishing every summer to fish the annual Striped Bass Catch and Release Tournament—and the tournament only lasts six hours. Each year I, and a group of similarly afflicted fools, rent a house on Lobsterville Beach for the week during which the tournament is held.

It's striper camp—deer camp on the beach if you will, replete with boats, beer, thousands of dollars of equipment, food that can be prepared in less than 30 seconds, and enough fly-tying vises attached to the dining room table to resemble a Sri Lankan sweatshop.

Lobsterville is the high cathedral of striper holes on the Northeast Coast during the last part of June. A huge crescent of beach with Dogfish Bar and the rocks of Gay Head on one end and Menemsha Pond, a huge bait factory, on the other, Lobsterville can be a fickle mistress, fulfilling your every desire one night, an exasperating tease on another, and an outright testosterone-crushing bitch when she wants to be.

There are ethereal nights on that beach when sunset brings on terrifyingly beautiful blitzes of crashing stripers ripping and tearing the water, gulls diving and screeching. Caught in the crossfire, millions of doomed baitfish leap out of the water to escape the sucking maws, only to be plucked from above. Set against the bloody pyre of the Menemsha sunsets, it is carnage at Mother Nature's best. When the sun disappears and darkness sets in, the selective feeding begins. Every cast brings the abrupt halt to the retrieve; the thrashing surface explosion and the steady first run out to sea. Hour after hour you stand knee deep in the quiet water; cast, hook up, and back up on the beach with bent rod pointing out into the shimmering blackness. The good fish will make you move down the beach to chase your backing. It's a game of musical positions as one angler is dragged down the beach into the dark only to be replaced by another that eventually disappears in the same direction, and so it goes from dusk till dawn. First light reveals a few haggard anglers, all with bent rods, standing exhausted, reeling now on autopilot. Randy, Pip and I had 130-plus fish one night. At first light I threw my gear on the sand and collapsed in exhaustion as Randy landed the last of his fish. I lit up a cigar and watched the sun push its way up through the sea. I couldn't tell whether I was drunk with exhaustion or pure disbelief at the night we'd just had. It didn't matter. Eventually we staggered through the unforgiving sand back down the beach to the house, the equipment came off in heaps on the porch and the house resounded with snores till early afternoon when the great hope of a repeat began again.

But these nights are rare and earned by other nights when the tides and the fish conspire to antagonize and demoralize, watching you trudge aimlessly in the soft sand from one end of that two-mile stretch to the other. It's part of the Lobsterville mystique—the difference between great fishing and no fishing can be a few yards and you'll never know it in the pitch dark until you find 'em.

"They should be here."

"Yeah, but they ain't."

"You think they're down at the bowl?"

"Maybe, but I sure as hell don't want to walk all the way back down there to find out."

"Well, they ain't here."

If you go they probably won't be there. If you don't go, it's guaranteed to be one of the great nights in Lobsterville history. It's part of the game. It's the fourth quarter.

"Damn. Alright, let's go." The sand gets softer and the waders get heavier—and more often than not the fish don't show on your little piece of the beach. Those mystical nights come at a cost.

The house we rent on the beach is a ramshackle two-story with a big deck overlooking the water. You can see the birds working from the deck. The sight of funneling birds in the afternoon has the same effect as throwing a rock at a wasp nest, creating a stampede of half naked, sleep deprived fools, swarming out of the house headed for the beach with fly rods in hand, stripping line as they go. They stumble over the detritus of a dozen guys unrestrained by work and wives—cigar butts, dirty clothes, empty cereal bowls, sleeping bags and gear—God, the gear. It's a semi-controlled disaster for a week. It's the reason women hate men—and ultimately part of the reason they love 'em. Somebody needs to take care of these fools.

It's the perfect headquarters for the tournament. I like this tournament 'cause it's loose. You can't really win anything except bragging rights. The prize structure, mostly rods, reels and stripping baskets, is raffled off at the breakfast the next morning to everybody that entered. Basically it's a chance for 300 fly fishermen to get together one afternoon, swap lies, go fishing all night and come back and eat a free breakfast and win a few prizes by sheer luck. It's good brainless activity. The premise of this tournament is pretty simple. You can win by catching and releasing the biggest fish or the most fish. The tournament starts at 7:00 p.m. on Saturday evening and ends precisely at 2:00 a.m. on Sunday morning. The committee puts all the names in a hat and draws partners. Your partner keeps your notebook in his vest and records your catches and you do the same for him.

I've always had good partners, pleasant folks who are a pleasure to fish with and have the same basic attitude about this thing that I have—let's just go fishing. The fact is I work for a major fly tackle manufacturer. That seems, for some reason, to initially impress the hell out my partners every year as if the fact I sit in front of a computer and write about fly rods makes me some kind of angling genius. I usually end up dispelling that myth by the end of the night when we haven't caught squat.

But this tournament brings out more than a few strange individuals, some of whom have either never fished, and ended up here for some reason at the behest of a friend, or are fanatical and have, as one once quoted "a burnin' in my ass to win this tournament." Our gang always ends up paired with at least one pathetic misfit. One year we had a Bee Gees look-alike complete with striped pants, a shirt with blowsy sleeves and a spinning reel attached to his fly rod. Sam just shook his head as they headed for the beach. This year Pip's partner didn't know you were supposed to have waders and spent the whole night running up and down the beach after Pip in Bermuda shorts and wingtips.

Everybody meets at the high school on Saturday afternoon and waits for the committee to draw the names. A few years ago it was 40 or 50 local guys and a few friends from off the island. Now it's well over 300 anglers from all over the Northeast who've taken advantage of the "excuse" and come to fish the tournament. The sponsors have their wares spread out over the yard and everyone peruses the latest piscatorial technology. Once we get paired up, my group grabs our entire cadre of partners and heads for the house. By 6:00 p.m. "headquarters" is full of not only our contingent, but all our partners as well. It looks like a staging area for a major invasion; chest packs and backpacks are strapped on, stripping baskets are adjusted and rods held at the ready as at least 20 anglers prepare to assault the beach. Rations are handed out—Gatorade, beef jerky and even a few Moon Pies (which I have to take credit for, being the only true son of the Confederacy in the house). Most everybody else is from the up this way, most notably Sam Talarico, a renaissance man if ever there was one. Sammy makes award-winning wine, is a world class photographer, and looks like Gabby Hayes after a good joint. Pip Winslow, a WASP prototype New England–bred entrepreneur, has *Mayflower* genes and his great-granddaddy was probably trolling for stripers when it came across. Matt Glerum is a certified genius who can converse legitimately on any level, but generally during this week concentrates on taking scatological humor to never before seen heights. And then there's me, whose only claim to fame is having once been responsible for protecting Archie Manning as an offensive tackle for the New Orleans Saints—and we all know how that turned out.

I've never won the tournament. As far as I'm concerned that's not the point. The point is that I'm down here fishing and this tournament is just the kickoff for one whole week of dedicated 24-hour-a-day striper fishing. I did come close once. I was standing with my partner up at Dogfish Bar when Sam came up and stood beside me to see how I was doing. He was loaded down with all his camera equipment taking a few hundred rolls of film for various and sundry assignments he had. I was throwing mighty casts far into the evening surf, trying to look real cool so Sam would take my picture and maybe I'd end up on the cover of a major fishing magazine. Hell, he's gotten everybody else on the cover so I'm just waiting my turn. (The fact that I'm big and ugly is beside the point.) Anyway, Sam put his camera equipment down and walks right up next to me. I mean he's about two feet away and shoots a cast right out next to mine. Now I've thrown about 30 casts since I've been standing there without so much as a tap and Sam threw one and *Bang!* Sam's line goes tight and the next thing I know he's running up the beach chasing this fish that's got him way deep into his backing. I finally see him stop about 50 yards up the beach and pull in this monster striper, which by the way ends up winning the tournament for the biggest fish. Well, Sam's screaming for someone to come take a picture of this fish for him as his equipment is right behind me on the beach, and I say to myself, "No freaking way." He takes the fish right out from under my fly, is going to win the tournament and he wants me to stop fishing and go take a picture of his fish. I don't think so. So poor Sammy sat there and yelled for help for a good five minutes while keeping this fish revived in the water. Me I just kept on fishin'. I remind him of that every so often. He owes me a cover.

This year Lobsterville was at her ego-stomping best during the tournament. We hiked that beach from end to end more times than I care to remember. Early on, I stopped casting for a moment to watch the sunset. As far as I could see in both directions anglers stood knee-deep in the placid water of the sound hurling hundreds of fly lines into the sea. The last light of the evening reflected on these gossamer wisps as they flew back and forth before landing gently in the water. It suddenly occurred to me that the fish were either dazzled by the array of taste treats being presented to them on this evening, or enjoying themselves immensely at our expense inspecting the myriad imitations being presented to them. Certainly on a night when over 200 anglers stand shoulder to shoulder and hurl lines and flies into the water it must look a bit like the circus has come to town to a fish who regularly cruises this beach for dinner.

This night my partner happened to be an older gentleman and by the time midnight rolled around he couldn't take another step. No fish were showing. We sat in the dark watching darkened silhouettes shuffle by in small groups. Suddenly the chopper appeared, painting the sea with a brilliant brush, searching for the boy. I watched this drama unfold, musing at the irony that in the midst of some 200 anglers a family searched vainly to find a lost soul. The boy was found the next morning floating in the bay.

My partner and I didn't catch any fish. In fact, I took him back to the house to await his son who was paired with a friend of mine. We sat and talked until the tournament ended in the early morning. I didn't mind not fishing. The crowds would leave the next day and Lobsterville would belong to me and my friends and the local islanders. The serious search for the night of a lifetime would begin tomorrow night.

The winning fish was 45 inches long. The highest number of fish was 69. Someone had found the schoolies. I didn't care. I don't want to catch schoolies. We later discovered a fisherman saved a man's life with CPR on the beach. A boy died that night in the dark water. I saw a partially paralyzed old man with a cane in one hand and rod in the other struggle his way up and down the beach in the heavy sand. Another boy with size 8 feet trudged up and down the beach for seven hours in borrowed size 13 bootfoot waders.

The next night I stood watching the water turn to fire in the sunset. Compared to the night before, the beach was empty. I thought about this turn of events and briefly pondered my mortality and the human condition—then a substantial silver tail slapped the water and swirled in the last light of day. I lifted a cast into the air and dropped it into the burnished sea and returned to more important things.

Life in General

Magic Beans

If there was one thing about farming in Vermont that was tough it was the fact that I was always home, a prime target for whatever or whoever drove in the driveway or called on the phone. During this period of my farming career Mimi was still working off the farm and I was left alone to fend off the purveyors of everything from magazine subscriptions to bulk feed and unfortunately if there's one thing I've learned in life, it's that I can't say "NO." You would think that at 6-foot-5, 280 pounds. I could stand up and tell somebody to hit the road, but instead I just stand there with a big goofy smile on my face and say incredibly intelligent things like, "Gee, that's great!"

For whatever the reason the idea of disappointing even the most obnoxious and total of strangers seems to create some dark anxiety from within. Perhaps I can blame part of it on my upbringing in which my sainted mother always taught me to be polite to anybody and everybody. This was, though, in the days before the insidious practice of telemarketing, which I believe was specifically designed to prey on unsuspecting southern boys with Baptist mothers. Ultimately these situations led me into the world of "magic beans."

Briefly defined, "magic beans" is my wife's code name for whatever predicament I happen to find myself in having been unable to say no. It's derived from that famous tale of Jack who was sent to town by his mother to sell their last cow and bring home money for food. Of course Jack was accosted by a smooth salesman and ended up coming home with a small bag of, yes, "magic beans." In my case these beans come in many forms. Perhaps a lifetime membership in a travel club for only $10 a month charged directly to my Mastercard—a particularly useful item for a dairy farmer who can't leave the premises for longer than an hour. Or perhaps a two-year subscription to the Cheese Snack-of-the-Month Club . . . major beans here.

Actually I'm not that stupid (hopefully). I can see a scam a mile away and if it comes in the mail, I laugh knowingly as I tear it up saying proudly to myself "Aha! You've got to be kidding." This is always within earshot of my wife to impress upon her that I'm not a total idiot.

The problem is when I am approached in person or over the phone. It's at this point when the man of steel turns to the man of Jell-O. I find myself completely unable to come up with a reason, any reason why I can't do this right now. It's as if I suddenly lose the power to speak. Like the time Mimi came home from the grocery store to find the house full of Jehovah's Witnesses that I had let in the door. When she walked in I was serving coffee and doughnuts and saying things like, "Gee, that's great!" I didn't want to be rude and figured if I let them have their say then they'd be on their way and I'd be off the hook. Mimi knew better and soon the traffic in the driveway was backed up like O'Hare with carloads of eager pamphlet-toting missionaries jockeying for position. When that first group left they must have jumped on the Witness hotline and called every one of their brethren to tell them they actually found somebody who would let them in the door, not to mention the fact they got coffee and doughnuts. Mimi is usually pretty good about helping me get out of some of these situations, figuring it's all a part of the "for better or worse" part of the marriage, but she refused this time. "You're on your own, pal." I did finally solve the problem for the next year or two by hiding behind the refrigerator whenever a car pulled into the driveway.

I now try to do better because I've discovered that saying no to someone I don't know is much the lesser pain than for instance trying to explain to Mimi why I bought a case of lightbulbs that are guaranteed to last ten years.

"What is this?"

"Uh, I bought some lightbulbs from this organization of handicapped people."

"That's fine, but why did you buy a whole case?"

"Well, she said they only come by the case, but they're guaranteed for ten years."

"Good, dear, but since we only have about twenty lights in the house and they're guaranteed for ten years, what do you plan to do with the other 180 bulbs?"

"Christmas presents."

Good, Bucko. Way to think on your feet. I've always had great empathy for Jack as I know exactly how he must have felt when he stood in front of his mother with that bag of beans.

My most recent bag of beans has been trying to explain to Mimi why we belong to Sprint, MCI and AT&T long distance services all at the same time.

"I told the guy we'd already switched, but then I couldn't remember which one we'd switched to. Then he said we were on his list of people who were supposed to switch and that they've been tracking our calls and that we could save a few thousand dollars over the course of a lifetime. Which one of these things do we have anyway? They just keep calling and telling me that they'll switch us for free and we'll have two months free long distance, no service charges, free maintenance, and all at half the newsstand price, plus a sports highlight video—oops! No wait a minute, that was the subscription to *Sports Illustrated*, but listen, I got you this great tote bag." I can clearly see the guy handing Jack the beans.

The great difference between Jack and I is that he planted those beans, crawled up the ensuing beanstalk, killed the giant and came back down a rich man. I, on the other hand, generally end up with just a bag of beans to show for my efforts and we all know the eventual result of hanging around beans. But I have learned a few lessons, and now when a salesman calls I do one of two things. If I'm alone, I immediately—before he has the opportunity to transfix me with his hypnotic spiel —scream loudly into the phone, "Quick, Nicholas, grab the fire extinguisher!!!," and then politely tell the guy he'll have to call back. Or if Mimi is at home I instantly hand the phone to her. "It's for you, dear." After discovering who's on the phone and giving me a wickedly dirty look, she then quickly and coolly carves that poor soul into so much chopped liver with abrupt and unmistakable authority. Definitely no beans here. I watch with unabashed admiration, wishing I had the courage to stand up and nail salesmen like that. When she hangs up the phone and strides confidently away, I simply watch her go, thinking to myself, "Gee, that's great."

Pass the Microchip Cookies

Vermont is a magnificent place to be. That's a given. You'd have to be real blind and partially stupid not to see what's around us. As a result, thousands of people come up here to visit, enjoy the scenery and exclaim to themselves, "Boy, wouldn't it be great if we could move up here, buy an old farmhouse and live in the country!"

Fortunately for those of us that do live here, most of them are not willing to give up the money they make down there and deal with the money they won't make up here. A good job in Vermont is a rare as grits at a New England inn. I've been up here now for 15 years and I just got my first real good job. I'm talking about a job that actually exceeds minimum wage and doesn't in some way involve firewood, mixing drinks, or plowing snow.

The job's pretty good, although after 12 years of various forms of self-employment and self-non-employment, it was a bit of an adjustment. I'm still having trouble weaning myself off that noon nap, and I've had to make some major wardrobe adjustments, but other than that it hasn't been too bad—until the other day when the part of the company in which I work underwent a large computer upgrade.

I guess I should have known the time was going to come when I was going to have to face the computer age, but living up here in the hinterlands, I just kind of hoped it wouldn't find me. I can see now that in order to ultimately escape it, I'm going to have to keep moving north somewhere far past the end of the power poles. Unfortunately Mimi didn't sound too enthused about the Northwest Territories.

I'm not talking word processors here. As lazy as I am, even I use one of those things 'cause it means I don't have to retype everything when I make a mistake, which considering I type about 50 words a minute with 50 mistakes is pretty helpful. Nope. What I'm talking about here is the real scary computer age where you interact with things named Quark and Syquest, and everybody talks in alphabetic gibberish.

"The CPU on my PC is not interfacing because there is a problem with the HD SC setup icon."—I mean what the H is that S? I obviously wasted 12 GD years learning how to spell.

Anyway, some guy named Chuck spent a whole week putting in all this stuff that we were informed will be obsolete by the time he gets it all installed, but that's just a fact of computer living. Then the Chuckster spent a whole day telling us how we could use this stuff to become more efficient, and another day running around trying to keep us all from crashing the whole system due to our enthusiasm at our newfound efficiency.

We now have systems that not only can talk to you, but you can talk to them and tell them to do stuff. No more pushing that heavy mouse around the ol' mouse pad. Now you can sit absolutely motionless and talk to computers named Bucky or Buffy or whatever the hell you want to name 'em. This little figure up in the left-hand window then interacts and does everything for you. Now, as I sit in the office I hear people in the next cubicle saying stuff like:

"Buffy, open Word files for Quark documents. Buffy, show invisibles." (I can feel the atrophy setting in as we speak). "Buffy, view by icon."

The upside to this is that it offers some exciting new possibilities in the world of office fun. My favorite pastime is now to walk around, stick my head in somebody's office and say things like, "Buffy, how's your sex life?" To which this cartoon character in the top left corner gets all flustered and starts saying "Pardon me! Pardon me!" I'm serious here, folks, she really does. You could really have some fun if you just stood up in the office and yelled "Buffy, delete!" Man, I bet you'd see some scurrying then.

Some of the other interesting upgrades are the e-mail and the Now-Up-to-Date Calendar. These programs link all the people in the office together into one complete interactive communications system. A large electronic body, if you will, controlled by microchip brain technology, functioning smoothly and crisply, sorting and disseminating information through the electronic pathways of life. . . . Anyway, if that's the case, I got dibs on being the stomach.

If I want to schedule a meeting, instead of going to all the trouble to lean over my partition and say "Hey Joe, let's have a meeting," now I simply have to put the meeting on the interactive public calendar, which will automatically update itself, alerting everyone that there is a meeting planned. I then send a memo by e-mail to all the people in the department I want to attend the meeting by going into the address book mode and picking out the people who I want to attend. When the message is sent it will then flash on their screen alerting them to the fact that there is a message. When they read the message I will be alerted on my screen that they read the message at which time I can then insert a reminder message that five minutes before the meeting will flash up on everybody's screen saying, "Get your butt to the meeting in five minutes." They can then hit the snooze button and the message will flash up on the screen every minute until time for the meeting, at which time they can tell Buffy to take a hike so they can attend the meeting. Piece of cake.

The only problem with this is when I get a message from somebody higher on the food chain than me, all the traditional excuses are eliminated. When I sit in front of my computer and the e-mail icon is blinking, I have to open it. Once I open it, then the sender receives a receipt saying that I opened it, so the always handy "I didn't get the memo" excuse is shot. It's also backed up on the public calendar, which won't let me use my spell check unless I open and check that thing. George Orwell would love this stuff.

I now have a computer full of things like Quark, Dyno-dex, CEToolbox, QuicKeys, Fontview and all these other neat words that mean absolutely nothing to me. What the hell's a quark? Somebody told me it means cottage cheese in German. They also use a lot of terms like ROM, RAM, and megabytes. The only Ram I know anything about has the word "Dodge" in front of it and "4x4" after it, and megabyte is generally how I like to eat pumpkin pie.

I hate to sound narrow-minded here, but this is all a little overwhelming to this poor boy. What worries me is the fact that these things have become so pervasive that if they crash, which they do with alarming regularity, everyone panics momentarily and then sit glassy-eyed in front of these blanks screens not knowing what the hell to do with themselves.

"My computer just crashed! My God, what am I going to do!"

"Quick, call the Applelink/AmericaOnline."

"NO! Download the Ascii files from the Compuserve Macintosh Database."

"Bucko! Quick, what're you doing to save your files?"

"I'm gettin' something to eat."

I think one of the things that scares me the most about this junk is my nine-year-old son understands it better than me. It's as if there was a computer chip automati-cally implanted into every child born after 1982. They can automatically pick up a flashing handheld computer game and play it without any instructions. In fact I've never even seen one that comes with instructions. I on the other hand pick it up and cannot for the life of me figure out what I'm looking at. I push the buttons and the lights flash. He pushes the buttons and the lights flash and the sirens, whistles and tunes go off immediately indicating that he has scored.

"Hey, Dad. I just won 145 to nothing."

I can just imagine sometime in the distant future when my grandson slides up to me in his automatic anatomical enhancer apparatus (commonly known as an "AAEA" or "double A" for short) and asks, "Grandpa, what was it like in the old days?"

"You young whippersnappers don't know how good you've got it, sonny. Why, back in nineties we used to spend hours pushing a mouse around."

"Gee! No kidding, Grandpa?"

"Yeah, sonny, it took a real man to run a computer in those days. In fact, the computers actually sat on our desks instead of being implanted."

"Aw Gramps, you're always kidding."

"So whaddya want to do this afternoon?"

"Let's go fishing!"

"Okay, grab the lazerrods and I'll meet you at the screen. By the way, did I ever tell you about when we used to fish in real water and . . ."

High Society

Recently as I was standing at a festive, gala, fund-raiser soirée to benefit something to do with art and culture, I watched the crowd and mused to myself (at these things I have lots of time to muse to myself) about social gatherings. Most people are thrust into one social environment where they tend to hang out because that's where they're most comfortable. Whether it's gliding glibly from conversation to conversation at the Southern Vermont Arts Center to the strains of Bach, or dodging flying beer bottles at Modell's out on the Atlanta Highway with Merle Haggard for background accompaniment—it's whatever makes you happy.

Somehow I've managed to stumble my way through a life that has put me into both these situations and a wide range in between. Not that that's any great achievement, but it does provide for some interesting comparisons.

My first introduction to polite society was at Grandma Moon's house when the Morningside Baptist Church Esther and Ruth Bible Class and Women's Missionary Society would gather on Wednesday afternoons. It was a mind-boggling assortment of orthopedic shoes, giant white pocket books and huge flowered hats arrayed throughout the parlor drinking iced tea and eating finger sandwiches and those little cookies all covered in powdered sugar. She'd come in the kitchen to find me standing over an empty plate with my face and hands covered in powdered sugar and my cheeks bulging. She would of course immediately forget what was going on and the Morningside Baptist Church Esther and Ruth Bible Class and Women's Missionary Society would get one hell of an earful from ol' Lula Virginia Henrietta Belle Woolfolk Moon. This was my earliest education at honing in on the source of the hors d'oeuvres and outrunning Grandma Moon's broom.

One good example of a social extravaganza (but not exactly polite society) is a University of Georgia football game. This is a rather large gathering in the 75,000 to 80,000 people range. There are some prerequisites for social success here: a large RV, preferably with air horns that play "Dixie," and a red and black color-coordinated wardrobe. Fortunately for Georgia fans, there is a wide variety of incredibly attractive plaids in red and black to match up with the wide red ties with the slobbering bulldog emblazoned on the front. (Imagine if you will a size 52XL red and black plaid blazer with matching pants. Scary, ain't it.)

Polite conversation consists of being able to yell "How 'bout them Dawgs!" with the emphasis on the word "Dawgs" and then being able to return that same greeting by yelling "How 'bout them Dawgs" with the emphasis on the word "'bout." This is key, as improper inflection is a definite faux pas. At the same time you must be able to politely carry on further conversation with a mouth full of fried chicken and a bourbon and branch water in one hand while leaving the other hand free to shake hands with everyone that is remotely familiar. Since you don't have a clue as to what their names are, you simply say, "How's it going theah, Bubba?" or put your arm around his wife and say "Hey, Sugar" (pronounced sugah) and be able to give her a kiss on the cheek without getting chicken grease all over her face or gettin' your eye poked out by her hair, which down there is generally lacquered to withstand up to a 30 knot wind factor. The fact that you don't know who the hell they are is perfectly acceptable as long as you make the effort to be cordial.

In comparison, I've noticed recently that "Bubba" and "Sugah" don't seem to work very well at the Southern Vermont Arts Center.

After my football days were over and I moved north and wandered into farming, most of my social gatherings were of the covered dish and potluck variety where conversations ran the gamut from how many come-alongs it took to pull that calf out of that cow, to the latest advances in manure management. Not exactly the stuff of chamber music and pâté (although pâté and manure are remarkably similar at first glance). I generally found myself most comfortable at Sherman's Store in West Rupert early in the morning when the farmers gathered for the morning coffee hour. It was an olfactory feast, the smell of fresh coffee, old store and barn creating a backdrop for conversations on government, taxes, heifers, deer hunting, whose hay was not cut yet, whose corn was not planted yet and whatever other daily problems confront the working farmer. There is a social ladder here. It is directly proportional to the work ethic of the farmer. Woe be unto the laggard who is late cutting his hay, which in farming roughly translates to attending a dinner party at Kathryn Graham's bearing a bottle of Riunite and a bag of ice.

As you might imagine, having played football for twenty years, dairy farmed for eight etc. etc., the opportunities to stand around with a glass of wine and a doily with one hors d'oeuvre on it have been few and far between. (By the way, it amazes the hell out of me how some of these people can nurse one hors d'oeuvre for about half an hour. The way they nibble at that thing you'd think they were hamsters. Just eat it! But I digress.)

Times change and I no longer play football or farm. I have a normal job and now live in Dorset, which has suddenly put me into an environment with which I am admittedly struggling to acclimate.

One of the problems I have in being social here is my size. This is not a physical crowd. It's not easy to maneuver 6-foot-5 and 280 pounds through a tight and polite crowd of well-dressed and coifed partygoers in a small room strewn with expensive antique furniture. Particularly when your entire life has been spent running into people at high speed or grabbing large pissed-off cows around the neck and holding on long enough to shove your arm down their throat to administer medication.

Anyway it seems each time I move I bump into somebody and then in retreating from them, bump into someone else and before you know it people are toppling like dominoes in an ever-widening circle around me. This problem exacerbates itself at the hors d'oeuvre table as when I'm feeding I tend not to pay attention to much around me. Occasionally I find myself leaning over some poor diminutive soul who scrambles to avoid being caught in the crush between myself and the crab dip. I therefore in the interest of being kind to my fellow gala, fund-raising soirée attendees have developed a strategy by which I can gracefully conduct myself at one of these functions, thus endearing myself to the hostess in hopes of being invited back sometime.

Basically it is a twofold plan by which I place myself with my back to a wall preferably near the kitchen door. This puts everything in front of me and prevents me from inadvertently backing up and crushing some poor lady's foot with my size 14 dress cowboy boots with the saddle bronc heel. Obviously I sometimes miss out on meeting some very nice people who never make it to my wall space, but better that than becoming acquainted with them with the opening line of "Oh! Excuse me, Sugah," as I'm picking her up off the floor.

The second part of the plan is the strategic placement of myself by the kitchen door. This allows me to intercept the hors d'oeuvre tray before it hits the room, both keeping me away from impending disaster at the table and giving me first shot at the shrimp puffs and pigs in a blanket (although I've noticed there is a serious shortage of hostesses serving pigs in a blanket up here).

This strategy can really pay off at catered affairs where waiters and waitresses are carrying trays of food around. If I don't meet anyone else during the night, I can assure you I will be fast friends with the wait staff before the night is over. Once I've established this relationship, the trays come to me first and as they go by I simply reach out and sweep about half the tray onto the waiting doily—a subtle technique, which I've developed and can now do quite deftly.

The bottom line here is people are social no matter where they find themselves. They seem to need each other and go to extraordinary lengths to gather their fellow humans around them. So the next time you see some huge guy over against the wall not looking terribly at ease, go on over and introduce yourself. Not only will he be mighty glad to see you, but he might share his hors d'oeuvres with you.

Big Boys, Big Toys

"Just think how much fun it will be."

"Paul, we can't afford it."

"Yeah we can, I'll give up lunches and everything." (Yeah right.) "That's about $200 a month. The kids will love it, and think of the romantic evenings looking at the sunset over the water" (while I'm fishing and you're making sandwiches).

"Just how much are you planning to spend here?"

"Just a couple of thousand dollars." (Seven or eight tops.) "I've seen tons of good used ones in the paper."

"And just where are you going to keep it?"

This question is always a good sign. It means she's come to the conclusion that this is going to happen, and sure enough, our family (me) became the proud owners of—The Boat.

Our family boat actually came our way as an indirect result of our dairy farm. When we sold the farm and moved to Dorset, we kept one tractor to landscape and help in the construction of the house. When all this was accomplished it seemed silly to me to have a big tractor taking up space in the driveway when we could have a big boat taking up space in the driveway.

Boat buying fever is essentially a disease to which there is no cure except buying a boat. Once you have the bug, it will not leave you until there is a large watercraft sitting in your driveway or resting comfortably attached to an incredibly expensive dock somewhere. This disease is not contagious, as other members of the family seem immune.

"Paul, I'm taking the kids into Manchester for their flu shots."

"Okay, I'll go with you and we can swing by Lake George and check out some boats."

"That's 75 miles in the other direction."

"I know. It won't take long."

At its peak it turns into a battle of wits.

"Hey Mimi, how about an afternoon drive with the kids?"

"Shhh!! Don't answer."

"I thought maybe we could drive out to Lake Ontario and check out some boats."

"Okay kids, both of you have strep throat. Got it?"

Eventually, however, the petty objections like money and "Have you ever driven a boat before?" are over-come—and there she is, 17 feet of fiberglass, teak and stainless steel with a hulking Mercury outboard loom-ing in the rear. Gleaming on her trailer behind the truck (which now has the $400 Class IV super hitch assembly and wiring harness), she is ready for the first day on the lake.

You can always tell a new boat owner instantly at the boat ramp. He's the guy with the car headed for the water and the boat headed up the hill. His wife is yell-ing at the top of her lungs—"Left, go left!!!" The little boy desperately needs to go to the bathroom and the teenage daughter is trying to make herself invisible. Each time he screws up he pulls a little further forward to straighten himself out and get a new start. Eventu-ally he ends up in the woods unable to move backwards

or forwards. Meanwhile all the seasoned salts standing around waiting are making rude comments about
this guy's manhood 'cause he can't back a trailer; as if
they've been driving Peterbilts all their lives.

Fortunately I didn't fall into that trap. No siree Bob.
One thing you learn to do as a farmer is back up. For a
number of years I spent a good deal of my time backing
hay wagons and manure spreaders hither and yon into
barns and under gutter cleaners so that backing a boat
trailer was a piece of cake. When I first pulled into the
boat landing, I whirled that truck around, pushing that
boat back toward the landing with pinpoint accuracy. I
could just hear the old salts murmuring their admiration for my backing skills. No manhood problems here.
I hopped out and swaggered back to the boat, undoing
the strap and the buckle, checking to be sure that everything was ready for launch and then hopped back
into the car thinking to myself, "Yeah boys, watch the
old pro in action." I then pushed it perfectly down the
ramp, launching it beautifully into the lake, watching it
drift effortlessly toward the middle—unfortunately with
nobody holding on, and as it happened, rapidly filling
with water.

"I think you forgot to put in the plugs," said the smirk-
ing seasoned salt.

"I knew that." Now just watch how good I can swim.

One of the things that people generally forget when
they're learning about a boat is the trailer. We were
headed for a week in the Adirondacks, the boat firmly
hooked behind the Jeep, a canoe on top of the Jeep and
the boat filled to capacity with float tubes, inner tubes,
skis, groceries, life jackets, suitcases, fishing equipment

and so much other crap that essentially our house was empty and we were in actuality moving to the Adirondacks for a week. Nothing like a week in the wilderness to renew the spirit.

"Mimi, what's that?"

"That's the laptop."

"The laptop!! We're going to the Adirondacks for crying out loud, what the hell do we need a laptop for?"

"It has all the kids' games on it."

"This is the wilderness. There's no electricity."

"It has a battery pack."

Thoreau would eat this up. But I digress. Here we go off into the Adirondacks and I'm personally feeling a lot like Tom Joad in *The Grapes of Wrath*. There's junk lashed to every possible rack and rail on the boat and the Jeep. Unfortunately the boat trailer was designed to carry the boat and not the household belongings of an average American family of four. About halfway there amidst a rousing chorus of "Row Row Row Your Boat" we are suddenly accompanied by thump thump thump your boat—a flat tire on the trailer. As luck would have it we happen to pull into the large parking lot of the Hillbilly Putt Putt course. Before the car limps to a stop, the kids are already out the door and headed for the putt putt course while I survey the damage.

"Well, Paul, you better get the spare."

"Uhh, what spare?"

"You mean there's no spare."

"Never thought about it."

"Where are we going to get a spare?"

"No problem. I'll just take the wheel off and go get it fixed and be back in a jiffy."

This of course meant unhooking the trailer, which I usually can do simply by picking the tongue up off the hitch and setting it down. This proved to be more difficult with three tons of kitchenware and furniture in the boat. It was just after I risked back surgery and a hernia lifting the trailer tongue off the car I realized I had no where to set it.

"Quick!! Get me something to set this on," I said, staggering from side to side, my face turning the approximate color of award-winning African violets.

Thinking quickly, Mimi grabbed the case of beer in the boat and plopped it on the ground and I dropped the trailer tongue, which immediately began the slow inexorable process of crushing the case.

"Do you think that will hold it?"

"I guess," I said, in a voice vaguely reminiscent of Chip and Dale.

When I left the parking lot for the first of about ten trips, there was my beautiful boat overflowing with crap, jacked up on one end, and semi-propped up with a case of beer on the other. Meanwhile my kids played about $85 worth of putt putt, as I spent the afternoon in search of a lug wrench, a new tire as the old one had disintegrated, and then someone to mount it on the rim, as of course no one seemed to be able to do all of these things at once. Ever notice that there are no actual gas stations anymore? Eventually I achieved my mission. Meanwhile back at the putt putt course, players complained of having their concentration disturbed by intermittent small explosions followed by the sound of spewing beer in the parking lot.

Getting used to a boat is like getting used to anything— it takes a little trial and error. Our particular boat has a large post in the rear topped by the rear running light. On Lake St. Catherine the only way into the main lake from the boat ramp is under a very low bridge. In fact everyone in the boat has to lie down on the floor, excuse me, the deck to get under it.

"Are we going to make it, dear?"

"No problem. See, it slides right" . . . Crunch!! . . . "under."

"Here, dear, you can tape this flashlight to the back."

This story really has no end. Boat disease goes into temporary remission when the boat is purchased, but eventually a more virulent form of the boat disease recurs—bigger boat disease. At this writing I am in the death grip of this malady.

"Paul, we cannot get a bigger boat now. You seem to forget, we are having another baby in September."

"Exactly my point! We need more room in the boat!"

Reductio Ad Absurdum

The other day I walked into the doctor's office for a routine physical and to my amazement tipped the scales at 319 pounds.

"Where the hell did that come from?" I said in feigned surprise, wiping the powdered sugar from the last doughnut off my sweater. "The last time I was here I was a svelte 285."

"Well, it's been a few years since your last physical and these things tend to slip up on us."

"Us? I don't see you weighing any 300-plus pounds." Then it dawned on me he was referring to me in the plural sense. I am now the equivalent of two people.

I don't think "slip up" was quite the right terminology either. I've been mugged by mass. We're talking Dallas Cowboyesque numbers here, the dancing hippos in Fantasia. My four favorite letters in the alphabet are now XXXL. I am legally obligated to pull over at weigh stations on the interstate.

But this weight business isn't my fault. (If overeating were a crime this would be the perfect legal defense for the nineties.) It was my upbringing, my environment as a child as it were. As both of my faithful readers know I was raised in the Deep South, the land of magnolias, beautiful women, exceptionally good football and deep fried food. If it's edible down there then by God it can be deep fried—and not in this namby pamby vegetable oil. No sirree! We're talking about good ol' all American deep fat fryers full of pig fat.

A prime example of a true good southern restaurant would be the Swamp Guinea down outside of Athens, Georgia. Here you can get all the fried catfish, fried hushpuppies, french fries and fried country ham you can eat for about six bucks. (The fried country ham is my favorite. We're talking a big chunk of pig here, cured in salt and dropped into a frying pan full of pork grease and cooked until it curls on the edges.) They lay it out on the table in big platters along with mountainous stacks of buttermilk biscuits dripping with butter that runs down your arm and quart bottles of ketchup (that would be the vegetable). Then you finish it off with a whoppin' slab of hot pecan pie and a couple of scoops of ice cream. (I always wondered if this place was owned by a greedy cardiologist.)

This type of cuisine didn't really take its toll in my youth practicing football twice a day in the simmering summer heat of Georgia and Mississippi, and burning enough calories in a day to make Jenny Craig disappear. It was not unusual to lose 10 to 15 pounds a practice and then go to the cafeteria and regain it immediately by eating and drinking something on the order of 10 to 15 pounds of food and drink. My favorite was tapioca night. I skipped dinner and just ate 10 to 20 servings of tapioca pudding and a couple of gallons of iced tea (the good Southern kind that's 75 percent sugar and deadly to diabetics).

But football had to end. Tapioca night did not. This struck home the other day when my coworkers started bringing in their leftovers from lunch and laying them on my desk without me asking for them. Apparently my reputation as a human disposal has preceded me. But alas, this is not, according to the American Medical Association, the way to live a long and happy life.

If we take a hard look at the food chain, all the crunchy, tasteless junk like carrots and celery are good for you and all the good, squishy stuff that melts in your mouth is bad for you. Wouldn't it be great to go to the doctor one day and have him say:

"Well, Paul, your tests have come back and in my opinion you're not getting enough doughnuts. Here's a prescription to Mrs. Murphy's. I want you to eat at least a dozen chocolate créme-filled a day until we get those cholesterol levels back up where they belong. I'm also going to recommend that each evening to reduce stress levels you smoke at least one good cigar and drink two fingers of ridiculously expensive single malt."

Wishful thinking.

So now it begins. The quest for the holy grail—my high school playing weight—250. The question is, how? I've done the Weight Watchers routine. This is where some perky size 4 who used to weigh about 900 pounds bounces around like a high-school cheerleader teaching you how to measure your food in portions that would starve a damn chickadee and drink so much water you need adult diapers.

"Okay class, today we're going to show you how to take one ounce of lean, skinless, boneless, meatless chicken and three green peas and make a delicious dinner for four. Or you can use one of your peas as a vegetable exchange and get a green bean!" All the while people in the class are running to the bathroom and hopping around in the hallway when someone else is in there. To top it off, you get the privilege of paying Miss Perky $10 a week to embarrass yourself on the scale in front of her and her little cadre of smirking, skinny helpers.

I've done the Neuropsychology of weight loss. Here you pay about $300 for six cassette tapes to play in your Walkman as you go through the day. A similar disgustingly perky voice tries to hypnotize you into believing that by eating nothing but grains and legumes you will become a fat burning machine rippling with lean muscles and sinew—somewhat like the horse who eats essentially the same diet. Mr. Ed with wicked bad gas—I don't think so.

There's now an $800 sweater-drying rack sitting next to the washer and dryer in the basement. It's called a NordicTrack.

"Excuse me, Paul, but what is this 800-dollar charge to Fitness World?"

"Well, uh, dear, that's my new NordicTrack. I'm really going to get back in shape and lose about fifty pounds. It's terrific. It has all kinds of electronic monitors that let you know if you're having a heart attack and everything! I can put on my Walkman and just work out for hours."

"Oh good, now you have somewhere to listen to your $300 tapes. It will be gathering dust in a week."

"No way, babe," I said confidently, climbing aboard the miracle machine. Mimi watched quietly as I shot one of the skis back into the sheetrock, and crashed forward on the stomach rest with my face, ripping out the heart attack gizmo wire that was clipped to my earlobe. She quietly walked away.

Then there's my personal favorite, the "eat anything you want as long as it doesn't have any fat" diet. This one was devised by the blonde with the really bad haircut.

"Paul, what happened to those four boxes of fat-free cookies?"

"I ate 'em."

"All four boxes?"

"They're fat free!"

"Gee, dear, you're absolutely right. Look. Zero grams of fat and only 4,000 grams of sugar. I can see you getting thinner by the moment."

So now what? What road to slightdom do I traverse? Wherein lies the answer to this lithe conundrum? How does Bucko, the Burgermeister of Bulk become Bucko, the Sultan of Svelte?

You know what? He doesn't. Where would Bucko be without a truck that sags to the driver's side? Who wants to read the musings of some undernourished pencil-neck geek? No, I owe it to my readers to persevere in my quest for ponderous perfection. Forget everything you just read. Gimme that pumpkin pie and don't bother slicing it. Bone Appeteat (*sic*).

In Search of Bucko

A few years ago, Bucko left. He just disappeared and left me sitting here wondering what happened to him.

For those of you who didn't know Bucko, he was a southern-born, grits- and collard-loving transplant who found himself snowbound in Vermont and wasn't quite smart enough to figure out how to get home. So he stayed here for 25 years, married, had three children, milked cows and then one day about six years ago he just up and vanished. For those of you who do remember Bucko and his Grandma Moon, his truck-driving dog Yoo Hoo, and the rest of his collection of misfits and misadventures, maybe you missed him a little bit. I have.

I can't say I blame him for leaving. For four years we spent every moment together, laughing at people, making fun of life in general and most importantly, poking fun at ourselves and our life in Vermont. Between the two of us, we managed to wreak havoc on what most people would consider everyday occurrences, but most importantly, we just enjoyed living here. There are few places on this earth where that statement bears any real truth.

Slowly though, things changed or I changed. I got so buried in the details of adulthood, fatherhood and fiscal responsibility that I lost sight of why I came here in the first place. I was here, but I simply missed the point and I went downhill from there.

One might wonder how that could happen, given the staggering beauty of this place. Even after 25 years, there are moments when these mountains and valleys suddenly present themselves in some new incarnation of color and light that triggers a smile of wonder. That smile inevitably eases into a slightly greedy grin, knowing this is my home and while thousands face the long drive home on Sunday night, I simply face the fireplace and a good book.

But, there came a time when even my glorious Vermont could not reach me. When that happened, Bucko disappeared.

At the very lowest point, even simple things became agonizingly difficult and those things that stir your soul suddenly had no meaning. I found myself watching my youngest child laugh and being completely unmoved. Chewing tobacco and pickup trucks offered no pleasure and my shotgun sat silent through the fall. Even the spectacular course of Vermont foliage season failed to dent this unwanted armor.

If you've ever known anybody with clinical depression, the hard part is understanding. The truth is, depression is simply a physical ailment no different than the flu. When someone is coughing and sneezing and puking all over the house, we feel sorry for them and try to comfort them without excessive gagging. When somebody can't laugh, can't smile or simply can't function, we tend to shrink away and wonder why they can't get a grip.

Truth is, they can't get a grip any more than the guy with flu can keep from crawling to the bathroom every five minutes.

But the real progress came when I sat down with the Mouse. I call her the Mouse for a couple of reasons. For one, she would probably fit in the game pouch of my hunting coat. When I was sitting on the couch (contrary to popular belief, you don't lie on it) she was sitting in her chair across from me, and she always took her shoes off and tucked her feet under herself. I realized the reason she did this was because her feet didn't touch the ground. The second reason had to do with my favorite fable, where the mighty lion was crippled by the thorn in his paw, and the tiny mouse pulled it out and saved him in exchange for his life. She was my mouse.

This diminutive little lady simply, through a series of discussions, pointed out what a bonehead I was and that my general course of thinking was a disaster. Certainly she, being the consummate professional, didn't couch it (no pun intended) in those terms, but in simple terms it was, "Hey, take a look around you for crying out loud."

A few months later, I had Yoo Hoo in the front seat of the pickup, the window was down and I was hauling ass down a dirt road singing "Sweet Home Alabama" with a big tobacco-stained smile on my face. I realized then, the Mouse had removed the thorn for good.

Since that day, I've thought a lot about Bucko. This Christmas, the Fersen family decided to drive to Atlanta for a good ol' southern Christmas and all the attendant insanity that makes Christmas in the south such a tribute to eccentricity. There was Aunt Kathy's frighteningly massive breakfasts, the ancient family fruitcake, and Aunt Ginny's house, a true tribute to excessive decoration. It was something we hadn't done in about five years. We packed the Suburban to the rafters with luggage, gifts, kids and took off.

Somewhere deep in rural North Carolina late Saturday night, the Suburban died on the side of the road. Eventually, the whole family was jammed in the front seat of a wrecker, lights flashing and the gift-laden Suburban resting forlornly on the flatbed, not unlike Santa's sleigh had he driven through Vermont during deer season. As the near toothless driver regaled my children, in some imperceptible Appalachian dialect, with tales of horrible wrecks and mangled bodies, we rumbled through the night toward a semblance of civilization replete with dysfunctional Waffle House waitresses, clueless mechanics and a jukebox with Elvis Christmas music. In the dim light of the cab, punctuated by the flashing orange light, I suddenly realized that sitting beside me, jammed between Mimi and I, was Bucko. He grinned at me and simply said, "Now we're talking."

We eventually made it back home, driving 25 hours through urban sprawl, a cacophony of neon and Cracker Barrel hell, dodging minivans and obese retirees in stupid baseball caps and brightly colored sweatsuits. At 3:00 a.m. on the New York Thruway, the road was a rolling mass of blinking red steel, slithering northward. Too many cars, too many people.

It was there, in the middle of the night, in one of those lucid moments of higher consciousness, brought on by excruciating fatigue and too many Krispy Kremes, that I was born again. You good Christians should remember when Paul on the road to Damascus gets hit by the blinding light and the Lord changes his life forever. Well, I was Paul on the road to Dorset and the blinding light was from a semi, and it wasn't the Lord speaking, but Bucko, telling me to get us the hell out of this mess and back to Vermont.

North of Albany the traffic thinned and by the time we reached Saratoga, only a few cars dotted the Northway. When I turned off, we were alone. We crossed the border into Vermont with the inevitable twinge of relief that greets our every return these past 25 years. The snow is a little deeper and whiter, the moon shadow of maples sprawled across the fields. There is no neon in Rupert, no urban sprawl in Pawlet, no mall in Dorset. The view from my hill still remains unabridged by other houses. I stumbled from the car, sucking in the cold of a Vermont dawn. Staring at the crystalline mountains, the stark birch grove against the dark hemlock forest, I wrote my name in the snowbank like a little boy with a relieved smile. Bucko and I had made it home.

From the Ground Up
A Few Words on Vermont Footwear

Twenty-five years ago I left grits, quail and red-eye gravy and took a drive north to the land of ruffed grouse, pot roast and potatoes. I told Grandma Moon I'd be back in a while, that I just wanted to experience a winter in New England. One wife, three children, a deer camp, two farms and a house raising and I'm still here. Grandma Moon has long since passed away and her farm dissolved into suburbia. Not much reason to go back.

In that time I've learned a few lessons, mostly by making the mistake first. Simple things like putting the shovel away after shoveling snow. Leave it lying and you'll be buying another one after the next snowfall just to find the first one. I did that.

There's antifreeze for gas tanks. Never heard of it. The first time my car was towed in, the mechanic said I need some dry gas.

"What's that?"

"Antifreeze for your gas."

"I may be from the south but I ain't stupid, gas don't freeze."

"Does here."

"Bull__t." I figured he thought I was some hillbilly rube and was on the verge of taking him to task when he showed me the container. As it turns out it's the condensation in your gas line that freezes and yes you do need antifreeze in your gas tank. Wait'll Grandma Moon hears about this.

Perhaps one of the more interesting aspects of Vermont I discovered is footwear. Back home I wore cowboy boots three seasons out of the year and in the summer I went barefoot. Barefoot and cowboy boots are not part of the Vermont footwear repertoire for good reason. I noticed the first winter I hobbled into Leo's (a former Manchester landmark) on frostbitten feet crammed into pointed boots, that everyone else was wearing big ol' rubber boots with felt liners called Sorels.

As an aside, Leo's was the best store ever in Manchester. When it died, part of Manchester's heart went with it. Where else could you get groceries, ammo, guns, clothes and shoes and buy a Jeep or get one serviced at the same place? I miss it.

Sorels were butt ugly, but once I put them on, their attraction was evident. Sorels are essentially a giant rubber boot lined with thick removable felt that makes one's foot look three times larger than it really is and after a while smell three times worse than it ever did. Given the fact that I wear a 14, my Sorels gave credence to the tale of the old woman who lived in the shoe. It also made me susceptible to provisions of the Clean Air Act.

Sorel enthusiasts are instantly recognizable, as their gait resembles a small child trying to walk in daddy's shoes and one of the intriguing sights in small-town Vermont is the daily winter commute of the working women from the car to the office. Beautifully coiffed and impeccably attired (yes, even in Vermont) they are the picture of femininity from head to calf until suddenly you come to the incongruous clodhoppers, which essentially make them look like thoroughbreds with Clydesdale feet. In their hands are the dainty slippers that will complete the lovely picture once out of the elements, but meanwhile they clomp down the street like children in the rain shuffling through puddles and muddy slush with gleeful impunity. Donna Karan meets Donnie Dorr.

Back then Manchester was a sleepy little ski village that had basically two seasons: foliage season and ski season. There were summer tourists and summer people, but for the most part it was fairly quiet. From March through July and from end of October to Christmas, a dog could take a nap on Route 7 and for the most part lie undisturbed. Shopping as a sport had not yet evolved. It was the skiers who introduced me to the another bizarre piece of northern footwear known as the aprés ski boot.

While worn a great deal in Vermont, in my 25 years here I have never seen an actual resident wearing a pair of these. This fashion statement is reserved for those who frequent the base lodges and night spots of the winter ski season. These boots are what we affectionately call the "dead dog" boot, because they look like someone crammed their feet inside two dead sheepdogs. Having never owned a pair (I am naturally suspicious of shoes with a French accent mark in the spelling), I've often wondered about the care of these boots and whether flea and tick prevention is necessary or regular combing and brushing is a prerequisite. Were a woman to complement these boots with a horned helmet and a brass brassiere, Wagner's Ring Cycle could very well be in the offing.

My third footwear discovery here in the north is the Vermont equivalent of going barefoot—the Birkenstock sandal. While incredibly comfortable, so I understand, and very therapeutic, they are undoubtedly the ugliest thing to adorn the foot since, well, since the Sorel. The Birkenstock is generally worn by those with left-wing leanings and organic taste buds who really don't care what they look like, which accounts for a very large portion of Vermont, as it were. I myself have not worn these because not only are they ugly, but my feet are ugly and the combined ugly factor would eliminate any chance I have of social interaction. Then there is the Birkenstock with socks. I won't even go there.

As I examine the present state of footwear in my family, I discover that I have evolved to hunting boots 95 percent of the time, the Vermont equivalent of the cow-boy boots of my youth, but most purchases now involve comfort as opposed to looks—a sure sign of aging. My older children wear flip flops year 'round, their desire to avoid laces (and any effort) far outweighing the pain of frozen, purple toes. I, on the other hand, have begun to look at sensible shoes. Before long I will be wearing thick soft soles with big Velcro straps and arch supports. Then come the bus tours. Damn.

Free at Last

Dan Mosheim and I sat in the driveway catching up. The discussion turned to kids and Dan told me of his son's new independence and his reliance on wood for heat. We both smiled knowingly at each other. Dan and I are both Vermont pilgrims having endured the great wood-burning odyssey that every Vermont transplant must negotiate. Coming up here as young men years ago, we both embraced that nec-essary self-reliance that imbues every pilgrim settling in the mountains: Gardens, wood heat, chickens, the whole self-sufficiency tableau enthralled so many of our genera-tion raised in the suburban fifties and sixties.

Being spring, it seems strange to be discussing burn-ing wood, but the truth is, spring is the most important time in the life of a wood-heating aficionado. The true wood burner knows that wood must be cut and stacked in the early spring to allow it to properly season by the fall. In fact, the true aficionado knows that great wood is seasoned two years in advance and therefore it is even more important to be ahead of the game.

Essentially the wood-burning pilgrim goes through four stages in life. Inundation, Resignation, Aggravation and Emancipation. The time varies, but the result is generally the same.

Inundation: When I moved up from the south, I was so enamored with the idea of wood heating that my first home was a converted deer camp on the back side of Stratton heated only with a woodstove and heat tape. The heat tape was there to keep the pipes from freezing because the woodstove died out at night and the temperature of the cabin would get below freezing (being a deer camp, it had no insulation). The dog's and the cat's water dishes would freeze and there would be skim ice in the toilet. Nothing more fun on a crisp morning than standing there melting the toilet ice.

I bought a $350 chainsaw to cut the wood and an $8,000 4x4 truck to haul the wood. I bought a big ol' splitting maul and reveled in my days in the woods cutting and splitting wood, hauling it back to the house and stacking it in preparation for the next winter's fury. My vision of myself in red plaid and big boots, keeping home and hearth warm and secure, came true. It took about four cords of wood to keep us warm during the season and nothing gave me greater pleasure than stoking the fire in my new stove. My wife spent most of her time wrapped in a quilt, and we used the 150-pound Newfoundland as a blanket, but I had arrived as a successful pilgrim.

Resignation: After three years of deer camp living, my lovely wife Mimi and I decided it was time to move to a more permanent home to have children and raise our family. I still believed firmly in heating with wood and even more so when I found the heating bill for the drafty farmhouse we bought was about $1,000 a month. Of course the former tenant was a 95-year-old woman who kept the farmhouse at near 90 degrees despite mild wind storms blowing through the windows. In fact, when we went to look at the house, both Mimi and I almost passed out from the heat. Some insulation work, a woodstove in the living room and a wood furnace in the basement solved the problem. That cost us about $6,000 and then I bought a $12,000 tractor and a $1,500 woodsplitter because I now needed 12 to 14 cords of wood to heat this wind tunnel. I spent hours in the woods cutting, splitting and hauling the wood from the woodlot to the house. My Bunyanesque vision of myself had given way to boredom and I found myself making up ribald lyrics to any song that came to mind while the damn chainsaw ruined my hearing. Meanwhile at the house I spent most of my time running up and down the cellar stairs feeding the monster in the basement that consumed wood like I consume pie. Endlessly. As the years on the farm progressed, the wood ran out earlier and earlier each spring, and a late spring snowstorm would have us burning old furniture we no longer wanted. In hindsight, Bus Mars auctions contributed a significant number of BTUs to my household.

Aggravation: By the time I built my house in Dorset, the only thing I liked about burning wood was the smell. I built a beautiful Rumford fireplace and out of sheer habit and frugality, I put in a woodstove as well, but I wasn't cutting any wood. It occurred to me one day that all the money I'd spent on cutting wood could have heated the White House for an indefinite period. My spring hours in the woods were now devoted to turkey hunting and fishing. The tractor turned into a boat, the woodsplitter into a nice side by side, the truck into a Suburban and the chainsaw is now relegated to light treehouse construction. I called my old friend Axel Blomberg from Rupert and had him dump a load of wood in the driveway, which I then paid my son to stack. I now enjoyed the ambiance of the fireplace and the woodstove with only the hassle of hauling the wood up from the basement.

Emancipation: After 10 years of hauling wood up the steps to the woodstove, enough was enough. Where once stood a glowing Resolute, now stands a clean-burning Jotul gas stove with real faux logs and embers that glow. The flames look the same (well, almost). To curl up in front of the stove on a cold winter's eve simply requires the flick of a thermostat and POOF! instant fire and heat. The dog curls up in front of it and could care less if the wood is friend or faux. The house is no longer enveloped in ash dust and the respiratory disease rate has plummeted. We still have the fireplace, which now is used ceremoniously on holidays and family gatherings. (I do draw the line at reading *The Night Before Christmas* in front of a fake fire.) At present my one cord of wood should probably last me about 10 years. If all goes well and I live the normal life span of the adult American male, I should need about two more deliveries from Axel in my lifetime.

Reality: I didn't mention this one. I have three children all of whom aspire to higher education. At present, between prep school and college tuitions I am burning equity faster than fatwood in a forest fire. By the time this is over and my children are brilliant and off changing the world, I'll most likely be back in the 800-square-foot deer camp with only wood for heat. That's okay. I didn't get rid of the old woodstove. It's still in the basement waiting for its return to glowing glory and I'm getting to that age where working in the woods again holds a measure of appeal that perhaps didn't exist 20 years ago. The chance to escape the inexorable onslaught of civilization is enticing. So if you happen to see an old deaf idiot cutting wood and laughing at his own dirty lyrics—that would be me. Just keep going.

Leaving the Fold

One of the great romantic myths is travel. I've been out there. There ain't nothing romantic about it. Having been out there, I can certainly understand why people travel here, but why in the world anyone would leave here to go out there is beyond me. Summer is a time for vacations and that means travel. Before you go, let me tell you what's out there.

I now travel a great deal because of my work. Somehow I've migrated from being a dairy farmer who couldn't travel more than an hour or two away on any given day, to a road warrior, a business traveler who now spends weeks at a time on the road going from coast to coast. I now have silver medallion status, five star gold status, quicksilver status, gold honors status—I've got all kinds of precious metal status which essentially means I travel too damn much, but better to have status than not. One who does not have status suffers greatly in the world of travel.

Generally I fly this one airline. They love status. The more I fly, the more they like me and do things to make me feel important. I now go to the front of the line at the check-in counter. I get the best seats on the plane. I get upgraded to first class. The other day some poor no-status guy was standing in a line of about 100 no-status people that were barely moving. You'd have to line these folks up with a tree to see if they had moved for the last 30 minutes. This guy, who was obviously going out into the world for the first time, chastised me for breaking in line as I stepped into the status line and was escorted right up to the desk. Total waiting time—10 seconds. I tried to be humble, but I just couldn't. I flashed one of my precious metal status cards that fill my wallet and smiled disarmingly, all the while thinking to myself, "Tough tea bags, pal."

I now belong to this airline's exclusive club. This means I get to hang out with other cool people of status. We get our own clubhouse right in the airport, and while the rest of the world pushes and shoves its way from concourse to concourse, drinks bad coffee and sits jammed together in naugahyde chairs, I sit in leather, listen to Vivaldi and thank the beautiful Asian girl for my freshly brewed Sumatran blend.

Occasionally I am forced to fly this other airline, due to expedience. I hate this airline. It was obviously founded by some guy who was always standing in the normal line and for some reason could never achieve status. On this airline, it is a race to see who can get the good seats first. Imagine a game of musical chairs except the players are all middle-aged. First of all you have to be at the airport three hours early to get in the A group. Any later and you're screwed. You'll be sitting in a middle seat between the two sweating fat guys. Once you get an A ticket you need to establish your position at the gate, which means you need to get all your coffee and reading material ahead of time, because once you get position you can't give it up. At first everyone is just sitting in the naugahyde chairs trying to block out the screaming of the infants and the incessant cell phone chatter, but secretly they're planning their move. Once the move is made, it's a jailbreak, so you have to be ready. Imagine 25 businessmen eyeing each other, trying to be cool and nonchalant, not wanting to be the first geek to get up and get in line, but making sure if someone does, they're ready. Ain't it wonderful how we never really grow up? Inevitably an hour before the flight, some idiot goes up and starts the line. You're done. Either you go up now and stand for an hour, or it's you and the two damp fat guys. I hate this airline. What a bunch of Marxists.

Generally I get a window seat, always in an exit row and often in first class (God I love status). Being just slightly smaller than a bull elephant, normal airline seats just don't get it. On the rare occasion that I am flying "the other" airline and happen to be late, and therefore at the end of the line, I get some measure of revenge and satisfaction walking down the loaded plane and watch the few people with open seats cringe and pray "Please not here, please not here" as I walk by. I pick my victim and slide into the seat, crushing him or her and therefore ensuring his or her discomfort for the duration of the flight. I smile inwardly. "That's what you get for flying this commie airline. I bet you'd have supported Act 60." (Inside joke.)

Anyway it is from comfort (or discomfort as it were) that I observe this country from one end to the other. From 30,000 feet it is a most spectacular place, but as I descend over the towns and cities, the stark reality of how most people spend their lives comes crashing home (bad choice of words). Thousands upon thousands of houses on tiny lots stretch down endless mazes of streets and cul-de-sacs as far as the eye can see. Occasionally dotting this Orwellian landscape is a giant mall complex. I've begun to notice that all these rat-maze streets ultimately end up in one of these mall complexes. Interesting.

It is at these moments that I'm inevitably stunned by the significance of Vermont. I've witnessed the destruction of Atlanta (Yankees just can't seem to get it right; first they burn it to the ground and then they come back a hundred years later and develop it into some unrecognizable, gridlocked, megametro, netherworld locked in consumer frenzy). The same in Phoenix, Seattle, central Florida (this will inevitably be mankind's worst legacy). For whatever reason Vermont has escaped this and it is emotionally evident to me every time I cross back from Salem, New York into Rupert, Vermont. The Lourie Farm, Sherman's Store, the Ceglowski homestead, the two old wooden churches, and as I head up over the mountain toward Dorset, my old farm.

So go out there on vacation if you must, but the truth is, these Vermont hills are the best the world has to offer. Want real status? Live here.

It's Just Labor Day So Far

It's autumn. Not much different from any other autumn, but I was sittin' here on my big ol' new porch we just added to the house and it occurred to me that I'm approaching the autumn of my years. It seems that we have over the years come up with a few colloquialisms that equate the length of our lives with the calendar year. Things like spring chicken, summer of my youth, autumn of my years, old man winter.

Figuring that I'm 55 and that I can expect to live to around 85, maybe 90, if I eat right and quit chewing tobacco—okay 85 max—this puts me somewhere in the very late summer of my years, or maybe the very early autumn of my years. I figure about the Labor Day weekend of my years.

When you reach the Labor Day weekend of your years, a lot of things start to change. For instance, you build porches on your house so you can have a place to sit and watch the world go by. As I look back, this was not a conscious decision on my part. I just felt like building a porch. Somewhere in the deep recesses of my evolutionary makeup, when I hit 55, my brain told me to build a porch. Up until now a deck was fine. Now I have a porch. I guess when you get older you need more protection. Something tells me in another ten years, I'll suddenly have the desire to enclose the porch.

Another thing that starts to happen is all conversations with your peers eventually turn to health. Go to a cocktail party of people my age and 90 percent of the conversations will revolve around ailments, prevention of ailments, cures for ailments, who has what ailment and ailments we have survived. This is natural as you approach the Labor Day weekend of your years, because the body starts to wear out. Not unlike my Suburban with 200,000 miles. It's still one tough, strong old truck, but stuff keeps breaking. Some of it you fix, some of it ain't worth fixin'. Biggest repairs I've had to date are a new transmission and a knee replacement. Those I took care of. The big dent in the side door and the receding hairline—who cares. Personally I'm tired of hearing about it. From now on, anyone starts telling me about their health problems and I'm walking away. Some of that stuff just ain't fun to listen to, particularly when they use words that end in "ectomy" and "oscopy." Sitting here on my new porch, I'm making a pledge to avoid all mention of health.

I got a piece of mail the other day from the AARP. The Association for the Advancement of Retired People. You've got to be kidding me. I've got two kids in college and a nine-year-old. I'll be able to retire when I'm about 85 and as we've already determined, I'll probably be dead, so quit sending me that junk. I've already determined my career path and when I get too senile to do what I'm doing, I'll simply go to work for Wal-Mart. Hell, they'll hire anybody.

I'm not looking forward to senior discounts. Thanks for the thought, but I'll pass. The last thing I want every day is to be reminded that I'm in the "we're going to give you a 10 percent discount because you're still alive" demographic.

I'm sure after my nine-year-old graduates from college and I'm living in a tent, I'll be grateful for this kindness, but for now, the first pimple-faced kid that looks at me and offers me the senior discount is going to be saying "Would you like fries with that" from inside the dumpster.

What is it about age that sucks the "cool" right out of you? Why are we destined to become staid, conservative individuals who make inane comments to our children because we think we're giving them sage advice? "You aren't eating right." "You're not getting enough sleep." "Don't wear that." We ate the same garbage when we were their age, stayed up all night drinking, drove drunk 'cause nobody cared back then, wore our hair down to our butts and wore platform shoes and bell bottoms for cryin' out loud. Our kids are so much smarter than we were it's ridiculous. I am convinced that one way to slow down the aging process is to LIGHTEN UP! Besides, look at what you're wearing—lime green pants with embroidered dogs, mixed plaids, and Rockport walking shoes. Badger the hell out of them about ethics and morals. There seems to be a distinct dearth of that in this world. Otherwise, leave your kids alone.

Finally there is the midlife crisis. This is where grown men (we seem to be a bit more conflicted here) suddenly realize where they are in life and go off half-cocked to try and regain their lost youth. The trick here is to avoid going from the sublime to the ridiculous in the way so many of us are compelled to do. Nothing is more indicative of aging than some old WASP with a toupee and some serious bling in a Miata. Get a hat and a Jeep. Forget the bling and get a puppy—much better chick magnet than gold chains on a middle-aged chest.

There is a fine line to graceful aging—not acting old, tempered with not trying to act too young. It's difficult, but here are some basic rules:

No bus tours. These exponentially accelerate the aging process through osmosis.

Your doctor's appointments don't interest anyone.

No alterations on the hair. You want to alter something, look at your gut.

No sandals. Old feet are ugly.

No sweat suits in public, particularly ones with wildlife pictures appliquéd on the front. You'll probably be kidnapped by a bus tour.

Your body no longer knows how to dance to rock music. You are not hip and cool anymore. Just ask your kids. Learn to waltz. It's beautiful and dignified and your wife will love you for it.

Stay in your house as long as you can. It defines you. Condos in Florida are stationary bus tours.

And finally, resist the urge to enclose that porch. Don't ever give in.

Winters I Have Known

It struck me the other day as the first snow drifted across the valley that I was no longer a boy from the south. I've been struck a lot lately by things that pertain to the journey of aging. After 50 we realize we're looking at less time in front than we have behind. We begin to get maudlin about the past and we ramble endlessly about the good ol' days. In essence at 40 we become our parents and at 50 we become our grandparents. Sitting there in the duck blind watching the snow drop in (the ducks were far too smart to do the same) I had one of these moments and realized I've spent more of my life in Vermont than in Georgia.

Doesn't sound very important, but to one through whom the indelible ink of southern blood still runs, it was a seminal moment. It suddenly occurred to me as the lone mallard of the morning set his wings and dropped his feet toward the river that I've made my life here. I was supposed to go back. I like grits.

I fired, the duck flared. Am I still a southerner? I fired again, the duck headed for Stuttgart. My dog was not impressed. I, on the other hand, was a man in conflict. I came up here to stay one winter and suddenly I find myself twice as old as the day I got here.

In that time I've learned a few lessons, mostly about winter, as Georgia winters require only a sweater to cope, whereas Vermont winters require a complete and complicated set of skills.

My first home here was a deer camp up in the national forest. Its only source of heat was a woodstove. At night the temperature in the house would often drop to below freezing as it had no insulation and the outside was plainly visible through the cracks. It was here I learned about heat tape. Not much heat tape down south. Basically it is an electrical wire that you tape to your pipes and then plug it in. It warms up and keeps the pipes from freezing. It was the only reason we could have plumbing in this cabin. First winter was going fine until one day the pipes froze. Come to find out a mouse had chewed up my heat tape. After agonizing days of no water and plumbing repair I went and got me a cat. Named him Brer Cat, an homage to Joel Chandler Harris, author of my favorite stories Grandma Moon used to read to me. As Mr. Harris might have written:

"Dis here arrangement wuz jus fine as Brer Cat he got's him a wahm spot by de fire, a nice litter box and de hoomin folks, dey ain't gots to use de outhouse no mo." From that point forward I had no rodent issues and Brer Cat lived with us for 10 years.

Had a cow named Icicle on our first farm. She was born in the barnyard on a howling cold morning and we didn't find her for a couple of hours. She was alive, but stiff as a corpse when I brought her to the house. Ended up thawing her out in the downstairs bathroom where she lived for a week. Certainly didn't have to worry about smellin' up the bathroom that week. Just blame it on the livestock.

Diesel tractors get so cold the fuel turns to jelly, and we had to build fires under the oil pan to get them started. Now that's a trick you need to be careful with or you'll end up being listed as a Darwin Award winner for blowing up yourself, and your tractor.

Tractor engine quit one day on the coldest day of the winter just as I was pulling out of the barnyard to spread three tons of manure. Took me two days and three fires to get it fixed and by that time I had a three-ton poopcicle sitting in the manure spreader. Took me two days and a bunch of fires to thaw that one out.

Twenty-seven years later, winter's still a bitch, yet I'm still here feeling smug and superior to newcomers who haven't endured the trials of rustic northern living as I have, and at the same time wallowing in southern persona. Damn! Which is it? Perhaps on good days I'm multifaceted and on bad days I'm schizophrenic. Who knows?

All I know is every time I go south, there's a distinct tug. I still like pork cracklins (deep fried pork skin with fat attached for you uneducated), fishin' with cane poles, grits and gravy and the open eccentricity of the southern culture, but for whatever reason, I'm still here in the land of maple syrup and frozen pipes. I tell people that after 20 years of two-a-day football practices in places like Athens, Georgia, and Hattiesburg, Mississippi, I never wanted to be hot again, but there's probably a bit more to it than that. I could find frozen calves in Minnesota and thaw manure in New Jersey, but I could only live in Vermont. The word alone is magical. There's two states up here whose very names invoke all that is good about the great north woods. Vermont is one, Maine is the other. I had to choose one.

For the time being my life is here and I can't imagine it being anywhere else. I became a man in the south. I became a husband and a father up here. I'm sure as age makes the cold unbearable, I will tinker with the idea of moving back south. Perhaps then I will write a column in a doddering hand for *Southern Living* about how wonderful it is to be in the south after freezing my butt off in the north, but for now, the cold just ain't that bad and I still can't stand being hot. Besides, real good pork cracklins are gettin' harder and harder to find.

My Space.com

Robert Frost wrote in his timeless poem "Mending Wall" of his neighbor's conviction that "good fences make good neighbors," though there were no cows to fence in or out. Colloquialisms abound in the English language about the need for space. "Absence makes the heart grow fonder." "Familiarity breeds contempt." There is an inherent need in all of us for space. Old Henry David did his best work when sequestered on his Massachusetts pond.

The fact is when I moved up here 25 years ago, the point of that move was to live a lifestyle with space. I don't want to see neighbors. I like them, but I don't want to see them. If I wanted to see neighbors, then any number of myriad suburbs in this country would be adequate. Then I could see Dick and Jane barbecuing every weekend in the next yard, behind their house that looks just like mine except the garage is on the other side. I could put up lovely curtains so that my bathroom window and their bathroom window, though a mere 10 feet apart, would be discreetly hidden. But the fact is, I don't want lovely bathroom curtains. I want to sit in my bathroom and look at the woods. That's why I moved up here.

But there is now an insidious trend sweeping across the land, and the world as it were, threatening my personal space. And that trend is communication. Not normal communication that is the foundation of society and the basis for how we behave, but communication on a massive scale that threatens to overwhelm us in a logjam of information that is too much for this lowly human to process. The frightening thing is that this has happened in just the past 10 years and it happened so fast that I was caught totally unawares until a few months ago when I went to Alaska. There on a salmon river, accessible only by floatplane and 250 miles from the nearest village, did I suddenly realize what was missing, or more importantly perhaps what should be missing.

What is missing is the time to think, to create, to let the mind wander into all the possibilities of what you could do, or what you should do. I realized at that moment that for the past few years, I had not had the time to do that. The reason: the barrage of endless communication that sweeps over me day after day at work and at home. E-mail, cell phones, Blackberrys, Internet, voicemail, hotmail, IM, text messaging. . . . For some reason, the more we can communicate, the more we seem to feel the need to communicate. The more we need to communicate, the more we expect response, so that now, lack of instant response is seen as some kind of miscreant behavior.

What if I don't want to talk to you? Does the fact that I don't return your call, or answer your e-mail, make me some kind of social pariah? The fact is, it now does. Over the years when someone said hello to you on the street, you were taught and expected to return a polite response. Now that most of the known world has the ability to say hello to you in an instant, you by centuries of social law are required to respond. Never did the founding fathers (more likely mothers) of etiquette envision this. It's like walking down Fifth Avenue at lunch and having everyone on the street say hello. Think about it.

When I travel, it is never more evident than in the airports and hotels, where poor souls struggle to get from place to place all the while in constant communication with someone somewhere. At some point I foresee a frenzied lemming-like event where we all go flying over the communication overload cliff, cell phones in hand, oblivious to the fact that we are falling.

The other day I stood in line to board the plane and next to me was quite possibly the most beautiful woman I've ever seen, in her mid-forties, perfectly attired and coiffed. A vision of loveliness. At a certain point she turned and smiled at me and to my shock and dismay on her ear was a silver contraption with a blue light blinking at me.

"Wow," I said disarmingly, "are you a real Cyborg?" She was not amused. It's bad enough that we carry the things, but now we are being asked to insert them in parts of our body so we can communicate with one person while we stand and communicate with another; or eat; or drive; or eat, drive, listen to music, carry on a conversation with the person in the passenger seat and talk to someone else at the same time. This is multitasking gone awry.

When a plane lands, it sound like an ice cream truck is coming down the aisle as multiple cell phones are turned on. God forbid these people have been out of touch for at least a couple of hours. Damn the airline regulations.

The other day I was driving my oldest son to college and his phone rang at least a dozen times in a two-hour period. He never answered, just popped it open and his thumb moved over the keys at light speed as he text messaged his friends with such scintillating prose as "c u n a wil." Translation: "See you in a while." I looked at his cell phone bill the other day and he had a mere 1,000 text messages for the month. That, my friends, is some epic communication. For his generation it is the norm. I cannot imagine what will freak him out in his old age.

This is scary stuff and it's come to Vermont, that supposed oasis of tranquility full of cows, green pastures, red barns and redder foliage. The poster child of the good life. The siren of rural values. But have no doubt, the electronic superhighway is here and the dirt roads of peace, time and tranquility are threatened.

So where does this leave me? I could rebel and refuse to use all these implements of massive missives, but if I do, I will be an outcast. Were I alone, that is exactly what I would do. I would gleefully take my electronics out to the gravel pit and admire the effects of 00 buckshot on a Samsung camera phone with text messaging capability. But I have my family to consider. I could no longer function at my job, communicate with my older children, and find out from my wife where I'm supposed to be at all times. In fact, I have been sucked into the vortex with the rest of you and no matter how hard I swim, I ain't getting out. The best I can do is tread water. The best I can do is grab my ten-year-old who has yet to succumb to the need to communicate with the world and take him fishing. For now he is my life raft and the one person in this world with whom I really do want to communicate. The rest of the world will come to him soon enough.

Dogs and Children

Dawgs

Reminiscences and Other Tails

L ife without dogs is like grits without red-eye gravy. You can eat 'em, but it's pretty damn boring. For you underprivileged out there who have never tried grits, trust me on this one. Anyway, for me, dogs bring to a life some emotional seasoning, those highs and lows of humor and tragedy that give our lives richness and substance.

The first time I ever remember crying for reasons other than scraped knees, or Glo Oxford swiping my toy truck, was when I saw *Old Yeller*. This movie laid my young emotions bare, and I cried every night for a week. Then of course came *Bambi*. It's my sincere belief that Walt

Disney got some perverse pleasure in killing off mothers and innocent creatures, but that's another story.

In any case a dog is such a loving, genuine beast that he brings out the most unalloyed forms of emotion from us. Some of the best laughs I've ever had in my life were the result of the antics of one dog or another. When we were trying to sell our farm over in New York, one couple looking at the farm was from Boston. It was immediately apparent that they had never set foot out of a metropolitan area. They were very quiet and reserved, ignoring all attempts at light conversation, which is what I do best. I'd spent the entire afternoon, sputtering around trying to find some common conversational ground and I was dying fast. They were immaculately attired in their obviously brand new "country clothes" from L. L. Bean, bought specifically for this foray into the "wilderness" of central New York state (notice how cynical I get when I don't like somebody). I was starting to get just a little fed up when my old Labrador, Beechnut, came over and sized up the situation. He sniffed around a little bit, and then proceeded to lift his leg and turn that lady's brand new, white tennis shoe a Day-Glo yellow. I don't know about her, but my attitude improved immensely.

There is a remarkable simplicity in dogs. There are no hidden agendas or ulterior motives in the canine relationship. They are the prototypical proponent of the golden rule, asking only in return what they unflinchingly give no matter how bad the circumstances. If you lose your job and are stricken with a fatal illness, worse still, your kids force you to buy Nintendo, or even, God forbid, you're booted out of the Field Club, Spot could not care one whit. My favorite philosopher, Chris, the

DJ on *Northern Exposure*, once said, "A dog is the purest form of unconditional love." That puts it about as succinctly as possible. In my wanderings, I've known some of the most miserable, useless excuses for human beings on the face of this planet. People who had all the redeeming value of a blackfly, but their dogs still loved them. That speaks volumes to the value of a dog.

Dogs have been man's faithful companion since the dawn of history and libraries are full of literature written about the relationship. Lord Byron was a great lover of dogs, one in particular. As an epitaph to his great Newfoundland, Boatswain, he wrote:

Near this Spot
are deposited the Remains of one
who possessed Beauty without Vanity,
Strength without Insolence,
Courage without Ferocity,
and all the Virtues of Man without his Vices.
This praise which would be unmeaning flattery
if inscribed over human ashes,
is but a just tribute to the Memory of BOATSWAIN, a
DOG,
who was born in Newfoundland May 1803
and died at Newstead Nov. 18th 1808

This is a soul stirring tribute, but having owned two Newfoundlands, raising one from a puppy, I know the destructive capability of a Newf puppy. It ranges somewhere on the scale between a fraternity party and a Tailhook convention. In my house, it was not a big deal, as I own nothing that cannot be replaced in Pawlet at a good

Bus Mars auction. But I wonder what the total damages were at Newstead Abbey, Lord Byron's ancestral home in Sherwood Forest? I have to smile and wonder if the troubled poet walked into his home to find the medieval tapestry, brought back from the Crusades, torn down and partially chewed, or if there was a small present sitting squarely in the middle of the hand-woven Oriental carpet that Marco Polo personally carried back from the Far East. Perhaps a Louis XIV chair with the leg gnawed off. Since I read about this relationship, I've often wondered if there will someday be discovered an unpublished poem by the eternal vagabond that will show that it's possible to cuss repeatedly in iambic pentameter.

For all their trouble, it's hard to dislike a dog. I've also found that it's hard to dislike a dog lover. Dog lovers are on the whole a pretty congenial group. One has to be if one is going to share a dwelling with a hairy beast whose idea of a good time is to ransack the garbage and chew large sections out of the rug. Dogs generally deposit a few bushels of hair on the upholstery, and find it amusing to stick their noses between your guests' legs, drool on them, or my personal favorite, use their legs as the object of their sexual desires. This is after they've tossed up some unknown organic substance they dined on in the yard earlier. Going to a dog person's house is always a relaxing experience for me, knowing that any faux pas I'm usually guaranteed to make has probably already been made by the dog.

I've had the pleasure of knowing quite a few good dogs in my life. One of my favorites was an old pound dog my fraternity brothers and I saved from the gas chamber. We brought him back to the "shack," which was our drinking and hell-raising spot out on the Oconee River. We dubbed him "Reeb," which is beer backwards, and he became an honored member of Sigma Chi. Reeb was a great icebreaker with the women. If you happened to be squiring a particularly lovely belle out to the shack, it was always good to have a dog around because women always get real mushy around dogs. (Hey! We needed all the help we could get.) Ol' Reeb witnessed the winning and losing of more than a few loves and many a graduate celebrated his triumph in the company of this gangly mutt. He was part of the college experience for a lot of people, and his name never fails to come up at every reunion.

There was another dog in my college life, UGA the Georgia Bulldog mascot. He had his own air-conditioned dog house in the shape of a huge red fire hydrant that was wheeled onto the field before every game. It was UGA who led us onto the field each week to the roaring chant of "DAMN GOOD DAWG! DAMN GOOD DAWG!" Then came that unforgettable moment when we were playing Auburn University for the SEC Championship and a chance to go to the Sugar Bowl. Both Georgia and Auburn were undefeated at 9–0. Tickets were going for hundreds of dollars and the Georgia campus was one big street party for the whole week. The classrooms were for the most part abandoned. We were ready to hit the field in front of 80,000-plus screaming Bulldog fanatics, all of us on adrenalin overload. The band that formed the corridor through which we ran onto the field began playing "Glory Glory to Old Georgia," and 200 trumpets blared the call to battle in my ears. The cheerleaders turned to lead us onto the field with UGA on his leash. I burst onto the field

with the team, the roar of thousands of wild-eyed crack-
ers rising in simultaneous crescendo with my desire to hit
someone. Paying no attention to where I was going, but
being swept along in the frenzied tide, I suddenly found
my legs all tangled up in UGA's dog chain, causing me
to stumble. I fought to regain my balance, but veered off
course and slammed into a flute player. Meanwhile UGA
was all bent out of shape and snarling at me—one of his
own guys. As it turned out my best hit of the day was that
unsuspecting flautist. Auburn won and I broke my leg in
the third quarter. Sometimes life is a bitch.

After I got out of college I was moving around too
much to have a dog, but when I finally ended up in Vermont, one of the first things I did was get one. One of the
reasons that Vermont appealed to me was that in this
area of the country, dogs are tolerated and privileged far
beyond the normal parameters of domestic dogdom. This
was an instant indication to me that people in the area
had their priorities straight. As evidence of this, one has
only to sit at the post office on a good day and watch as
every other car that drives in has a dog sitting in the passenger seat, or lying in the back of a pickup truck. They
hang out in the entrances to stores, they even frequent
the occasional restaurant, which I'm sure freaks out the
health inspector, but that's part of the charm of the area.
I'm relatively positive that nobody ever died from eating
near a dog in Vermont.

I myself like big dogs, real big dogs. Dogs are generally
a reflection of one's personality and lifestyle. Being big,
as I am, it would seem a bit ridiculous to me to own one
of those pocket-size fluff balls that yip all the time. They
of course are fine as a companion for some elderly lady

in an apartment, or perhaps as a mascot for the local hair salon, but for me, any dog that requires a sweater to go outside ain't of much use.

I've owned two Newfoundlands, Rhum and MacDuff, both of whom were in the 150-pound range. Both stood about 36 inches at the shoulder with long coal-black coats and huge heads that gave them a bearlike appearance. In fact, one time in the parking lot at Stratton I overheard a skier, obviously from deep in the center of Manhattan, pointing out to his son the tame bear in the back of the truck. I of course regaled them with the tale of how I had found the cub in a blizzard back in the national forest. It was all going great until Rhum opened his mouth and barked.

When Mimi and I got married we left my visiting mother in charge of the cabin and MacDuff while we went on our one-night honeymoon. It was the dead of winter and that old deer camp had no insulation and the snow on the roof melted during the afternoon and ran down into the door jambs. The next morning when mother went to open the door to let MacDuff out, she found both doors frozen shut. There is nothing as impatient as a 150-pound dog that needs to go outside. He began to whine and throw his considerable bulk against the door as my poor mother chipped away at the door frame with an icepick, wondering what in hell she had done to deserve this. Nothing in her previous 65 years of genteel, southern living had prepared her to be trapped in a deer camp, on a frozen mountainside, with a rampaging bear imitation with his legs crossed. When she finally did get the door partially opened, MacDuff opened it the rest of the way, tearing off the upper hinge as he dove outside. Mother said there was an audible sigh of relief from the woods.

These days, Labs seem to be the dog of choice in the Northshire, as I would wager there are more Labs per square mile here than in any other part of the country. Perhaps it has to do with the great hunting tradition in this area fortified no doubt by the Orvis influence. A short perusal of the retail store will reveal the ubiquitous Labrador on everything from keychains to andirons. Whether this is a function of the number of Labs among the landed gentry, or one of the reasons the breed is so popular (the chicken or the egg?) is unclear, but what is clear is that if you own Labradors and want to decorate your house in the sport dog motif so popular in this area, there is no shortage of decorative accoutrements.

I myself now own two Labradors and a pound mutt, but my house is done in the aforementioned Bus Mars auction motif. We find with three dogs that this is a better arrangement, as dog-worn furniture is easily and inexpensively replaced with a quick trip to Pawlet. Beechnut is the grand patriarch of the family who at 12 no longer has to abide by the rules of the house, but instead makes up his own. He comes when called only if it is to his advantage, as in dinner. If it's to go outside on a cold winter's evening, he simply puts his head back down and returns to his nap, oblivious to the entreaties of his "master."

Bo, the pound mutt, is a paranoid schizophrenic borderline psychotic who at a certain voice level will proceed to whiz all over himself. This was not a big problem until we installed the wall-to-wall carpet upstairs. Now whenever Bo is to be admonished for some misdeed, he must be quietly and sweetly enticed down the stairs until he is safely on the wooden floor where one can scold him at will, sponge and mop in hand.

Then there's old truck driving Yoo Hoo, who is also my faithful hunting dog. When we get into the woods it's his job to scout the area in front of me and scare up some birds. Generally, though, he stays right by my side and when I give him the signal to hunt, he looks up kind of sheepishly, and slowly rolls over on his back to get his tummy scratched. Some huntin' dog. Needless to say, I don't take him on any group hunts.

I, for one, from this point on could never see a reason to be without a dog. I do believe the good Lord knew what he was doing when he gave mankind the canine. We are, as a species, the most pathetic group on this planet. We kill each other for no reason, we pollute, and yet oblivious to these heinous acts, we are unconditionally adored by our dogs. Certainly they have their faults—one has only to look at the trampled flower beds, the dead spots on the lawn, and the bottom of your shoe—but that's a small price to pay for a companion who's glad to see you every day, any day, no matter what you've done. If there is a human being on this earth that can match that performance, I have yet to encounter them. Not countin' you, Mom.

Suffer the Little Children

I just recently again became a father. Jackson Cooper Fersen is a sturdy young man who is the spittin' image of his big brother Nick and grandly named after a Civil War general and my best fishing buddy on Martha's Vineyard. With my first two named with opulent and traditional family names, it was time to inject a little new blood into the Fersen family name archives—a little Bucko if you will. The lad weighed 10 pounds 13.7 ounces and upheld the Bucko tradition of siring the world's largest babies. For that I apologize to no one except my dear wife to whom I apologize profusely.

So here I am once again embarking on that never-ending journey of nurturing and caring for a human being created by Mimi and me. A beautiful child who will be the light of our lives and cost us roughly half a million dollars to raise by the time he finishes college.

This makes three children, so estimating one and a half million dollars to bring up these children, at my present salary I can retire when I'm 148. But be that as it may, I'm looking forward to raising Jackson, as the two I have are for the most part pretty decent.

Parenthood is a remarkable experience. It is our job to take these little people and teach them all the important things they need to know to get through life—all those things about which we ourselves have absolutely no clue. But it is our job as parents to fool them into thinking we know what we're talking about and therefore they will listen to us. At least in theory. In actuality, our children are smarter than we are the minute they're born and it's due to their exposure to us that they become fraught with fault and stupidity until eventually they end up just like us. Children when they are born have no fears. They get those from us. When they are born they aren't mean, they get that from us. When they are born they have no desire to go to McDonald's, they get that from us. The older we get, the more simple-minded we become until finally it is our children that are taking care of us and so on.

Nevertheless we persevere. In the course of raising these children I have learned a few things about myself, the most important being that I learn more from them than they will ever learn from me. One of the biggest mistakes we make as parents is trying to make our children and our family unit live up to our own image of what they should or shouldn't be. I'm probably more guilty of this than anybody, as my poor children will attest.

Take for instance the Fersen family holiday season. Were it up to me we would temporarily change our names to Currier/Ives for the months of November and December. Frozen food, microwaves, Oscar Mayer lunchables and other twentieth century food groups would not be allowed. Everything would be baked from scratch. This would of course be expensive when you add in the medical bills from Mimi's January internment in a rest home. The house would be decorated with natural greens to the extent that the dogs would think they were still outside and whiz all over the furniture (a small price to pay). The children would each receive one gift, which they would cherish, and perhaps a sled to share. They would run up to me and say something along the lines of, "Oh, thank you ever so much, Father" and I, lighting my pipe, would sit in front of the fire and bask in the warmth of the season.

But it ain't up to me. Try as I might to impart some old-fashioned Christmas value into our household, my children are on the cusp of the twenty-first century while their poor father is mired in the nostalgia of the nineteenth. As much as I would like to think I can protect them from the evil electronic empire, I can't (and probably shouldn't). Christmas morning is filled with the sounds of bleeps and blips, mountains of presents are scattered from one end of the house to the other and my children say things like "Cool!! This rules!!" Looking back I would imagine my poor sainted mother viewed the invasion of the television the way I envision the invasion of cyberspace. Each generation has its demons. But my kids can program the VCR and the remote, they can run any computer, solve the riddle of the most intricate computer games; and the Internet, for me a dark and terrifying trail with road signs like http://www.@ubvm .buffalo.edu (I mean what is that?), is for them a brightly lit path to knowledge. They are comfortable in a future in which I'm not. They are smarter than me.

Another test of the parent/child relationship is sports. Having achieved total mediocrity in the NFL, I promised myself when my kids came through the ranks of pee wee sports that I would calmly watch and encourage them, allowing them to progress at their own pace and achieve the best they could achieve on their own. Think again. This lasted until the first time my son stepped on a lacrosse field at which time I Jekyll and Hyded right into a screaming lunatic. At each and every game I promise myself that I will remain calm and not display any idiotic histrionics that might embarrass myself, my poor wife and particularly my children. This lasts until the first time Nick gets the ball and heads downfield for the goal. I suddenly find myself taking each step, making each move and, what's worse, yelling instructions at the top of my lungs as I sprint down the sidelines with him. You would think I had enough athletic competition through 21 years of football, but nothing in my experience has ever raised my competitive hackles like watching my son on his field of endeavor. To his credit he still claims me as his father and admonishes me mildly. "Gee Dad, it'll be all right, settle down." They are more mature than me.

Parenthood is teaching by example. We are for the most part imperfect creatures. We make mistakes on a regular basis, yet it's our job as parents to correct and try to prevent mistakes in our children. The remarkable thing is our children seem to wend their way through our foibles and understand most of what we're trying to impart while at the same time watching us do exactly the opposite. Generally I find that when I'm telling them to take their clothes upstairs from the laundry room, I'm standing in my underwear in the laundry room—where all my clothes are. Their rooms are significantly cleaner than mine because they can't tell me to clean my room. At the same time I'm making them sit and do their homework, I'm trying to think up a reason to tell Marsha the esteemed and ever lovely editor of *Stratton* magazine (think that'll work?) why my column isn't done yet. But, to my children's credit, they seem to understand the things that are right and forgive me for the things I do wrong. They are more tolerant than me.

The bottom line is as we stumble and fumble our way through parenthood we will learn more than we will ever teach. They will tolerate my ranting and raving about what they should and shouldn't do and sometime in the future they will sit back and laugh about how Dad used to get dressed in the basement.

They'll pass on their knowledge and their goodness to their children—and probably a few faults they picked up from their dear old Dad. But I'm sure a few less because they're better than me.

Travails with Kids

There has always been for me a great attraction to the road. Of the many careers I have had, there is one I haven't and still to this day dream of someday doing— drivin' the big rig. Imagine sitting up in that big cab looking down on the world, shootin' the breeze on the CB and heading for the horizon astride that rumbling diesel. YEEEEHAH!! Oh well, maybe someday.

Still I can come fairly close by getting in my big Dodge Ram and hittin' the open road. Alone with my thoughts (or lack of), the hum of that massive V8 as it consumes huge quantities of fossil fuels, the sounds of Hank Williams on the stereo and the company of a big hand-rolled Dominican, the blue smoke rolling over my face like a scented veil; these are the handmaidens of a testosterone high, and I am, in my mind, but a few clicks from the big rig.

But those mystical moments come fewer and farther between now as over the past few years my buddies, solitude, old Hank and that big cigar have been replaced by Mimi, Nicholas, Elizabeth and now Jackson Cooper. This isn't a bad thing overall; in fact, in the general scheme of life I consider myself one of the luckiest men in the world. Somehow as the consummate underachiever, I've managed to stumble my way into a life with a beautiful wife and three relatively magnificent children (give or take an adolescent hormonal eruption or two). Anyway, bottom line is I still get to ride around in my big red Dodge, but now I'm surrounded by a gurgling baby, two contentious siblings and a wife, bless her heart, who has stomped a hole in my dashboard putting on the imaginary brakes when I get too close to another car. Not exactly a testosterone prolific environment.

Case in point. Recently we went for a week sojourn in Atlanta where the majority of my family still resides. As we are not overly wealthy and the cost of five plane tickets would feed and clothe us for the next twelve years, it was decided we would drive. A mere 2,000 miles round trip with two adults and three kids in the front of a king cab pickup truck. The open road, the adventure, the romance, the endless concrete ribbon stretching before us, the bickering, the happy-meal action figures, the singing dinosaur tapes in my stereo, the loaded diapers in a close environment. Possibly the defining moment in this scenario is when I find myself at a truck stop next to a big, beautiful, midnight blue Peterbilt. The driver, replete with really cool, old worn-out cowboy hat and a mouthful of Redman chewing tobacco is sitting there watching me clean Jackson Cooper's butt with a baby butt wipe and change his diaper while strains of "Cuddly little dinosaur" come wafting out of my stereo. I even had on shorts and running shoes. Damn!! What a geek.

It's truly amazing to me the amount of junk a family of five can manage to bring along, particularly when one of those five is ten months old. (Actually it's four

people as I, being the father, don't get to bring anything.)
Each of the children got to bring a huge duffle bag, a bi-
cycle, a large L. L. Bean canvas tote the size of a bushel
produce basket full of toys and games, a blanket and a
stuffed animal. My wife had a number of bags packed to
the rim with "necessities," and then came the baby. The
child weighs 25 pounds and he's packing 400 pounds
of luggage. First, a full complement of incredibly "cute"
outfits for each and every occasion when he would be
presented to some new contingent of the family. Then
there was the giant tote full of formula and baby food,
the toy bag, the diaper and accoutrements bag, the crib,
two strollers (one formal and one informal) and finally
the folding space jumpy. I got to bring a toilet kit and
a pair of spare underwear that my son Nicholas let me
stuff in his bag.

Eating on the road is always an adventure. We packed
a bunch of coolers full of food to save money, but we
kept stopping at fast food places to get all the different
game pieces necessary to win a million dollars. You
would think that I, as the head of the household (actually figurehead; my nine-year-old daughter in reality
runs the family) would put my foot down and say no,
but I was hoping against all odds to win the million dollars so the next time I could buy plane tickets for the
whole family, hopefully on different airplanes. Since we
were there we had to eat and fill the car with prizes, toys
and other happy-meal detritus.

I particularly love the handy drive-through feature.

"Mmmmfmtkemmmf ymmmfr ordmmffr?"

I assume that means she wants my order.

"Ah, yes, I'll have a number two meal combo with a Coke."

"No, Daddy, I wanted a Sprite!!"

"Ah, make that a Sprite."

"And I wanted it supersized so I get the game pieces and the Hunchback of Notre Dame action figure!!"

"Okay, make that supersized."

"Dear, the action figure is an extra $1.50," states my practical wife.

At this point I don't give a damn.

"Fine, and now a Jolly Roger meal with the chicken doubloons and a small milk."

"No, Daddy, I wanted a chocolate milkshake!"

"Sweetie that doesn't come with the Jolly Roger meal."

"But I want a milkshake."

"It's all right dear, I'll drink the milk and she can have the milkshake," chimes in my accommodating wife.

"Okay, give us the Jolly Roger meal with the doubloons and the milk and then add a chocolate milkshake and I'll take the number five Rancho Deluxe combo with a iced tea."

"Lmmmf mmfin tmmf tea?"

"Ah, yes."

"Bacmmfon mmmfph Mmmfcho Zztuxe?"

"Ah, no."

"Mmmmf zzop?"

"What'd she say?"

"I think she's asking if you want ketchup."

"Sure."

"Chmmfse?"

I look at my wife again, who seems to be able to interpret electronic jive.

"Cheese, dear."

"Yes."

"Anymmmphffhting elfftse?"

"Wait a minute. What do you want, dear?"

"Oh, I'll just have some of yours."

Damn.

"That's it."

"That'll be mmfpiut, ninetymmghtfive."

I drive around and hand her a twenty and get back a few small coins. Then we ended up with three milkshakes, two chicken doubloons, no Rancho Deluxe and two more Quasimoto action figures. Being trusting souls (or just stupid) we don't discover this until we're already headed down the interstate.

Now we're talking true testosterone depletion. I'm in my big ol' pickup speeding down the highway with a cab full of screaming urchins, I got a couple of Quasimotos poking me in the butt and three or four more sliding across the dashboard, a baby spittin' creamed spinach on my upholstery, and a mouthful of chicken doubloons. What the hell possessed somebody to make monetary units out of chicken?

It was at about 750 miles that we hit critical mass. The inside of my truck looked like a terrorist blew up a McDonald's, the baby just filled another diaper and the conversation in the back seat went as follows:

"He hit me!"

"She was annoying me!"

"But he won't give me back my calculator!"

"I had it first!"

SCREEEEECH!!

"All right, that's it. Out and start running!!"

"Dear, you can't make the kids run down the road."

"Watch me. Out and start running. I'll tell you when you can get back in."

"But dear, they'll be exhausted."

"Duuh!"

It was reported that somewhere near mile marker 126 in North Carolina a young girl and boy were seen running down the side of the road being slowly pursued by a large red Dodge pickup. Strains of Hank Williams were heard wafting from the cab of the truck and the driver was grinning from ear to ear, tossing what appeared to be small figurines out the window and enjoying a very large cigar.

Release the Hounds

It's autumn. The trees are slowly suffocating their leaves in the rubescent ritual that is foliage and the wind whispers the first hint of brutality. For the hunter, it's wait's end. For the dogs in our lives, it's show time.

Pickett, my chocolate Labrador, will be four this season, having first opened his eyes in July of '02, but already a veteran of three seasons. The first time I saw him was the day I picked him up at a kennel in Colorado in mid-September having sent a deposit sight unseen on pedigree and parents' pictures alone. His first act for me was to retrieve a toy mouse and bring it proudly back to my feet, drop it and look up with the expectation of yet another round. Sold.

Now to get him home. I was not about to stick him in the cargo hold. I found out that given his size, he could ride with me in an under-the-seat kennel. Fortunately he was too young to understand these kennels are generally reserved for the use of well-coiffed and bejeweled women with smarmy, aloof cats or little dogs that yip. Dogs shouldn't yip. Pickett came through the experience unscathed and with his hunting genes intact. On a side note, if I ever need to find another woman in my life, I will simply go to an airport with an eight-week-old Lab puppy. As my son so ably puts it, "a sick chick magnet." Translated that means I was surrounded by adoring women the minute I hit the door with Pickett in tow and the flight attendant even moved me to an empty seat in first class. His first day he was already taking care of his master.

Going through security I set off the alarm and had to be searched. Since Pickett couldn't go through the X-ray machine in his kennel, he had to be searched as well, the assumption being, I suppose, that at eight weeks he could storm the cockpit and eat the crew. I stood there in the standard search position with arms out and Pickett sleeping comfortably in my outstretched hand, five feet above the floor. He woke just long enough to relieve himself in my hand, leaving a puddle on the security footprint pad, much to the consternation of the security guard conducting the search. While I am forced each flight to remain silent and accept this degradation, Pickett expressed my sentiments exactly and was, from that moment, my dog.

There are good dogs and then there are great dogs. Pickett seems destined for greatness, at least as it applies to my relationship with dogs. I've had good ones, but none who've responded to me like this one. I've come to the conclusion that much of this has to do with me, having chosen Pickett at this particular time in my life when my patience is at its zenith and age has cast its mellow spell. I no longer fret over unfulfilled expectations and as such my dog and my children have exceeded them. Funny how that works.

Pickett is a marvel of breeding and genetics. Over the centuries his forbearers developed a propensity to chase (retrievers), while other dogs developed the desire to stalk (pointers) and others the desire to herd or guard or yip as it were. Dog anthropologists have come to the conclusion that dogs as a species are only about 15,000 years old, an infant in the grand scheme of evolution. Man did not domesticate the wolf as most people believe. The dog self-evolved when man stopped being nomadic and settled into villages. The village dump became an instant and easy food source for certain canine-type species. The ones that had the least fear, ran the shortest distance when confronted with man, and returned the quickest, began to interbreed and evolution accelerated exponentially, creating a creature comfortable with man. Thus the dog. The prototype of this first dog is called the "village dog" and from these dogs came all the breeds we now know, including young Pickett.

Hard to believe that the dogs we see strutting and fretting around Westminster all evolved in a mere 15,000 years from a few dogs hanging out at the dump. I would

imagine that some French poodle named Chevalier
would be as disgusted with the notion that he evolved
from dump dogs as some people are about being descended from apes. Not exactly Adam and Eve in the
Garden of Eden, but Pickett has no such notions of gran-
deur. I bet if I let Pickett loose near a dump, he'd probably think he was in the Garden of Eden. I'm not quite
sure what it is about Labradors, but they have a propensity to eat anything as long as it can be swallowed and
even then they're up to a challenge. Old Yoo Hoo, the
now deceased and famous truck-driving dog of years
past, once ate an entire sofa save the frame. For Pickett,
a frozen cow patty is just as much fun as a Frisbee and
a lot tastier to his mind. Over the past four years he's
eaten three pairs of reading glasses, two remotes, two
pillows, numerous boots and shoes, a jar of peanut butter, a lacrosse stick, three or four golf balls and many
other items too numerous to mention (not unlike the
listing of a Bus Mars auction). Remarkably he lives to
tell the tale.

This hunting season Pickett will enter his prime. His
first year he sat inside my coat and watched the festivi-
ties with great interest and by the sixteenth week of his
life dragged his first duck back to my feet. By the end
of last season he was charging through ice strewn rivers
in search of his game, entering the water with Herculean leaps and reveling in the boat ride home, his coat
covered in ice and frost. I have loved all my dogs, but
this one seems destined to be the one I will remember
most.

A few years ago I wrote a short introduction to a dog
catalog for my company. It was before I met Pickett, but

it seems prophetic. Of all the things I've ever written, it is my favorite.

We aren't house-proud. If we were, we wouldn't abide the scratches on the door-frame, the holes in the screen, the darkened shine of worn spots on the chair. We would wince at the mottled carpet and fret at the hair clinging to our clothes.

We don't. If anything, we lovers of dogs are a tolerant lot, finding greater value in the unabashed affection of our friend than immaculate sofas. Shoes can be replaced, but heroic retrieves are timeless.

Without dogs, our houses are cold receptacles for things. Dogs make a fire warmer with their curled presence. They wake us, greet us, protect us, and ultimately carve a place in our hearts and our history. On reflection, our lives are often referenced in parts, these parts defined by the all too short lives of our dogs.

Pickett's life will most assuredly be a reference point for the best part of my life.

It's Spring!
Why Am I Still in this Hockey Rink?

One might wonder why for a spring magazine, I might choose to write about hockey. It's because I'm still sitting here in this oversized chest freezer watching my youngest play his forty-fifth game of the interminable season known as hockey: A marathon of frozen mornings and ridiculously bad coffee made by inept parent volunteers at rinks throughout the region.

Where I grew up and was semi-educated in southern public schools, this time of year meant azaleas and dogwood, girls in tank tops and cut-off jeans cut way too short (as if there were such a thing) and convertibles with the top down and a cooler of beer in the back. If anyone had told me that 30 years later I'd be sitting in a walk-in freezer watching a bunch of ten-year-olds try to decapitate each other, I'd have told 'em to lay off the wacky weed and pass me another beer. But here I sit, bad coffee in one hand and the other hand gripping a hand warmer in the pocket of my Arctic parka.

Whereas soccer lasts about a month and a half in the fall and lacrosse lasts about the same in late spring, youth hockey begins in mid-autumn, continues through the dark of winter and emerges still going strong in the light of early spring. St. Patrick's Day will still find you and your weary compatriots staring blankly at each other in the "warm room" after a two-hour drive for a 7:00 a.m. game in the nether regions of eastern New York State. "Warm room" is a euphemism for the lobby of the rink where the temperature is generally slightly higher than liquid nitrogen. In one rink, the cream and sugar was outside the concession window. I had to get out my knife, cut open the carton and carve off a chunk of cream for my lukewarm coffee (true). If I get up that early and stay that cold for the entire day, at least I should be duck hunting.

To be fair, youth hockey is rather wonderful when your four-year-old takes his first tentative steps on the ice, leaning on the stick for support, his jersey reaching down to the top of his skates. He and his teammates shuffle like geriatric midgets, trying to stay upright at the same time they are attempting to get the puck into the net. Of course, at this stage there is no concept of spacing and position, so the puck is constantly surrounded by ten little hobbits desperately trying to stand up and actually hit the puck with the stick. There is, in my experience as the parent of three athletes, nothing more heart-warming in the world. Then they get older.

First there is the equipment. A few hundred dollars for skates, stick, helmet and pads, all of which they will outgrow in the next week or so. At the beginning of each season we all go to the basement and pull out last year's equipment only to find that our children look like Li'l Abner in pants and pads four sizes too small and skates that fit like the glass slipper on Cinderella's ugly stepsisters: Back to the hockey store.

Of course any equipment will not do. The older they get the more sophisticated they become as to what is cool and what is decidedly not. Skates must have the Integrated Wedge technology or the G-Force Cushion fit system in order for them to be able to properly skate. Sticks must have the correct flex and curve, just like the pros, who by the way are the only people who can actually flex these things or know what to do with the curve. All of this is packed into monstrous bags, larger than the children and heavier than most Volkswagens, under the weight of which the children stagger like drunken sailors returning from leave with their sea bags over their shoulders.

Then there is the tape. Massive amounts of athletic tape that is used to hold up shin pads, tape the handle and the blade of the stick, re-tape the blade and handle of the stick and then re-tape it again so that the puck comes off the stick at a particular speed and trajectory, or so they would love to believe. Generally they are lucky if they hit the puck, but we love to live our children's fantasies with them so we buy the tape, tons of tape. Enough tape so that one season's worth if stretched end to end would reach from somewhere in Quebec to somewhere in Saskatchewan (good hockey places).

Each weekend during this interminable season, we get up with the cold blue dawn, get in the car and head for hidden hockey rinks all over the northeast, slowing down only long enough to grab yet another breakfast combo as we whip through the drive-through; the hockey parent diet is considered second only to smoking as a coronary risk factor.

Inexplicably, people feel the need to build their hockey rinks in the most out of the way location possible, so that parents from the opposing team can't find them. Take a look at our own Riley Rink. If you didn't know better you'd think you made a wrong turn and were headed for the cement factory, until at the last second a road appears on the left. Still can't see it from there. We went to one rink up in northern Vermont that was so remote, everyone spoke French and a wrong turn found us stopped on a dirt road, talking to Lucky Pierre of the Canadian Border Patrol.

This of course is where some idiot decided to hold a state-wide tournament. Part of qualifying for the tournament was being able to use celestial navigation to find the place. We did, though, have a nice lunch in Canada in-between games.

Nothing is more fun than following the poor parent who has been designated to lead the caravan of SUVs and minivans full of smelly equipment, sleeping children and bleary-eyed parents in the quest for the elusive rinks. If you ever see eight or nine minivans making wild and dangerous U-turns across four lanes of traffic, one behind the other, rest assured it's a hockey team that is lost and the leader of the pack is now the object of derision and foul language from those behind him who believe him to be a total moron.

There is a particular affliction among the hockey faithful that because of the skating skills and stick skills needed to become proficient in this game, their children or the children whom they are coaching should spend every waking moment on the ice, throughout the year, playing for select teams and going to endless camps in order to ensure that they eventually end up in the NHL. I read once about a family who logged over half a million miles in this quest. Ahh, the delusions with which we parents burden ourselves. The fact is, perhaps one out of 200,000 of these little hockey hobbits is going to actually make it to the NHL. The other 199,999 are simply at some point going to turn their attention to other things, and rightly so. If my little one makes it to the NHL, it will be his decision. I'll be glad to log half a million miles, but it will be because he asked me to, not because I wanted him to.

A Few Words Before You Go

Seems like just yesterday I was slowly driving down the shoulder of the highway, while my two older children were running in front of the truck. They'd been misbehaving in the back seat and I finally, kicked them out and told them to start running. Ran 'em till they were exhausted and didn't hear a peep from them the rest of the trip.

Now they're in college and getting their revenge, as I'm destitute. What they don't yet realize is that the price of this fabulous education they're receiving is I will demand a corner room in the nursing home with two windows. But of all the things I've done in life, raising these children is the thing of which I'm most proud.

Now they're getting ready to leave the fold and head out on their own. So the chances for me to impart wisdom and guidance are coming to a close. Therefore I am putting together a list of things they should know before they leave. It is as follows:

Read a book a week for the rest of your life. Doesn't have to be *War and Peace*; some of the best books I've ever read took a couple of hours. If you live to be 80 and start at 21, that's 3,068 books. Start with everything John McPhee ever wrote and that in itself is equivalent to another college education. Then read Thoreau. We could all use a little Thoreau right now.

Credit card companies are the modern day equivalent of colonial indentured servitude. The only difference between them and loan sharks is their suits are a bit more tasteful. Their usurious rates are the same and their intentions are the same. Pay your credit cards off each month. If you can't, you're living beyond your means.

Dress up when you travel. Nothing is worse than sweats and tank tops on an airplane. Have a little self respect.

Tattoos are okay. Just plan ahead and remember they will be there forever. Look at your Mom and Dad now. Would you really like to see a rising sun coming out of the back of our pants? Chances are it would now be a setting sun and a pretty sad one at that.

Learn the difference between "effect" and "affect." I get e-mails all the time from supposedly intelligent and highly placed businessmen who instantly lose credibility with that one. The effect of misusing "effect" and "affect" could affect your career. Speaking of e-mails, write a letter. You really want to impress someone, sit down and write them a letter, in long hand, on good stationery. It's a lost art.

Don't do anything for the money, do it because you love it. If you love it, you'll be good at it and the money will follow. As for money, the more you have the more you think you need to spend. Spend it on experiences, not possessions. Possessions are the antithesis of freedom. Imagine yourself as a sailboat running before the wind and possessions as anchors. You figure it out.

If you find yourself standing in line in front of a box store all Thanksgiving night in order to save a couple of hundred bucks on anything, it's time to reevaluate your life. When much of the rest of the world is standing in line to get food and medicine for their children, that holiday ritual is obscene.

If you make a lot of money, buy a big, beautiful piece of land; build a modest house in the middle of it, 1,000 square feet per person maximum. Anything more is ostentatious, environmentally detrimental and a waste of money. If you need more room for your stuff, you've got too much stuff (see above). Take that piece of land and donate the development rights so it stays intact forever. It will be the greatest gift you can give your children.

Always own a dog and an old truck. Forget the cats. Dogs love to ride in the front seats of old trucks, cats don't.

Never compare yourself to anyone else. In every case you will feel superior or inferior and neither of those is the truth.

Eat oatmeal every morning for the rest of your life and go fishing as much as you can. Your Grandma Moon did both and she lived to be 96. She fished till she was 94 and had oatmeal the morning she died. Also learn to eat grits and love 'em. It's part of your heritage. Lots of butter and then smash 'em up with your fried eggs. Nothing better.

Buy one new car in your life, just to say you did it, and then never do it again. It's the worst investment there is. New car smell ain't nothing but carpet glue. You can now buy it in a spray can. Buy used and then find a good honest mechanic and make him your best friend for life.

Virtual reality isn't reality. The time will come very soon when you can do anything from the comfort of a chair. Get your butt out of the chair and do it for real or don't do it. Take at least two weeks out of every year and go somewhere where Blackberries are something you pick and Bluetooth is the result of eating fresh blueberries. Leave the computer and the cell at home and don't be accessible to anyone except the ones you love.

Marriage is not mandatory. There is only one reason to marry and it has nothing to do with money, prestige, society, convenience or tax breaks. If you want to get married, do it somewhere extraordinary, like the Galapagos. I'll pay for that. I'm not paying for a $5,000 cake. Ain't no cake that good. You want flowers? Pick some.

Don't have any children on my account. Have 'em because you want 'em. Then be prepared to do nothing else for the next 25 years. Support them, but don't indulge them. Make them earn their way, just like I made you. You turned out pretty well.

Farming

A Farmer's Christmas

The morning chill of an old farmhouse greeted me when I tossed off the covers. It was quarter to five, and I congratulated myself for not pushing the snooze button on the alarm a second time. Rummaging through my pile of clean clothes in the corner, I gathered my outfit for the day. Then I turned to my dresser and pulled out a pair of thermal underwear.

"Most definitely need these today," I thought to myself.

The house was silent and I peeked in on Nicholas as I do every morning. He had kicked off the covers as usual.

"Merry Christmas, buddy." I pulled the blankets around him and headed for the stairs in the darkness.

Beechnut's rhythmic snoring was the only sound as I reached the bottom of the stairs. I opened the wood-stove, pulled the coals forward and threw in a couple of big chunks. Beechnut's head rose, glanced my way as if to say "about time" and then dropped back to the old blanket that was his bed.

"Tough life," I chuckled as I turned on the stove for the first cup of coffee.

It was five now. It's only the first couple of minutes in the morning that I dislike. By the time I'm downstairs and the coffee water is going, I feel good. I feel like a farmer. I am a farmer, but it is this time in the darkness of early morning when I really feel like one.

Before going to the barn, I looked into the living room at all the presents displayed around the tree. The big pedal tractor, "just like Daddy's," stood prominently in the middle of all the other toys and gifts. Plugging in the lights, I stepped back and watched them twinkle. Hopefully, Mimi would be able to keep the children upstairs until I got back from the morning's milking. The face of a child on Christmas morning, particularly my child, is one of the absolute joys of life.

The chill in the bedroom prepared me for the cold when I stepped out the back door. Secure in my thermal underwear and with steaming coffee in hand, I trudged through the crunching snow in the darkness, knowing each step by heart. There was no light over the mountain as of yet, nor would there be for at least another hour. It came later each morning.

The cold gave way to damp warmth in the barn. There is no heat in the barn except that generated by the bodies of 45 cows. Even on the coldest of nights the barn is a comfortable 40 to 45 degrees. A glance at the inside thermometer confirmed that. The outside thermometer read eight below. Perfect Christmas morning.

With only the night light in the far corner, the girls were just two rows of massive shapes outlined in the shadows. They didn't move too much when I came in, just an occasional glance.

"Merry Christmas, girls." One head turned back to look.

"Guess you wouldn't want to take the day off, huh?" No movement.

"Didn't think so." The maternity pen was in the far corner under the night light. I moved there quietly to check on Cindy. It was her time and she had done her best to warn me the night before with her rapidly filling udder and her tail cocked at an unusual angle. I looked in the pen and she was standing there with her tail still awkwardly positioned. She looked up as if to say "not yet" and then turned and faced the other way. I watched for a few moments. Her body stiffened and she shuddered. A good contraction.

Not long now.

I flicked the light switch and the barn was flooded with light. Immediately there began a heaving of flesh and the clanking of metal as 45 cows began to throw themselves forward in order to stand up. In a moment they were all staring down the middle aisle where I stood with the grain cart. Cows are wonderful creatures of habit and one of the secrets of dairy farming is maintaining a consistent routine. As for these cows, when the lights go on, they know it's time to eat.

Dinah—six, Gretchen—five, BB—five and a half, Magic—six. The grain chart is in my hand, but I rarely look at it, feeding the cows from memory, being now as much of a creature of habit as they are. Amazing what the mind retains from simple repetition.

I scraped down the alley behind the cows and threw on a fresh layer of sawdust. The milking machines were brought out and hung up in preparation for the beginning of this morning's ritual. The udder wash was steaming in the bucket and it was 20 minutes after five. I had only to flip the switch to begin, but it was not yet 5:30.

This was one of my favorite moments each day. I stood in the feed alley and leaned against the wall looking down the row between the cows. Every head was down and the low, pleasant sound of munching was accompanied only by the occasional clank of the metal stanchions as the cows reached out farther for more food. It was bitterly cold outside, but in here it was warm and the smell was of fresh sawdust, sweet hay, and cows. A satisfying odor for one who loves this life. The fact that it was Christmas morning only served to make the moment even more satisfying.

The last swig of coffee went down and I walked over to check Cindy before getting started. By this time she was down on her side, pushing hard and peering back over her flank trying to watch the process of birth. A contraction forced a low groan from her and she became momentarily rigid. She relaxed and breathed rapidly. Walking around behind her, I waited for another contraction. It came and squeezed her sides until two small hooves appeared momentarily.

"Well, that's good." I decided before I got busy with the milking to make sure the calf was in the proper position and there were no foreseeable problems. Rolling up my sleeves, I washed my hands in the iodine solution we used to wash the udders prior to milking. I stepped in the pen quietly so as not to upset Cindy's efforts. Kneeling behind her, I gently pushed my hand inside her past the two small hooves.

"Somewhere here, girl, there ought to be a nose." Moving my hand up the spindly leg, I suddenly bumped into the head.

"Yep, here she is." I pinched the nose of the calf and it jerked back instinctively. A good healthy calf in the right position. I smiled to myself.

"Okay girl, I'll leave you to your business." I pulled my hand from the warmth back into the comparative chill of the barn.

"This is what you have to look forward to, little one." The machines were attached and I moved methodically from cow to cow, washing, prepping, taking the machines on and off, spraying the finished udder, with cleanser. The radio played Christmas carols from across the barn, accompanied by the pulsing hiss of the milking machines. Usually in the mornings, I leave the radio off and enjoy the quiet solitude, but the strains of Christmas added just that much more pleasure to the security of the barn on a cold morning.

The milking was over and the cows again munched on the second feeding of the day. It was close to 7:30 now and the thought of pancakes and sizzling bacon, as well as the cries of delight from Nicholas's discovery of Santa's treasures, pushed me to finish the final chores in a hurry. I headed back through the barn and stopped to take one last look in the maternity pen before leaving for the house. Cindy stood with her head down and underneath her sandpaper tongue was a tiny brown creature that was all ears and legs. She was wet and shivering, but under Cindy's careful attention, she would soon be dry and comfortable. I threw a shovel of sawdust in to absorb the moisture on the floor. Cindy looked up, "No problem." The calf made its first awkward attempt to rise, but Cindy pushed it gently back to the floor and continued to lick the calf dry. "Wait till I've finished, little one." I walked back toward the house. The sun was just beginning to show itself over the mountains to the east. To the west, the dark blue mountaintops were beginning to lighten to pink. There was no wind, no clouds, the smoke from the chimney rose straight up into the morning sky. It was cold. Very cold and very clear. The only lights in the house were the Christmas candles in each window. Nicholas's light wasn't on yet.

"Good, I didn't miss it." So far it had been a good morning, a normal morning, but a good one nonetheless.

Maple Syrup

One of the numerous advantages of living in Vermont is proximity to that golden elixir of spring, maple syrup. But even living here, this nectar of the north woods is not cheap, though you will find somebody will undoubtedly give you some in repayment for one good deed or another. I've received syrup for changing flat tires, chasing cows, pulling someone out of a snowbank, and a host of other reasons. It's a Vermont maxim: When in doubt, give maple syrup.

When I moved to Rupert, one of the first things I noticed on my farm was about 15 huge maples along the road. Having not yet become used to having an abundance of maple syrup around, I was enthralled with the prospect of producing my own. The question was, being absolutely ignorant about the process, how could I turn the sap from those trees into maple syrup? I found two good sources. First were the local producers in town who were more than willing to give advice, and second was an invaluable book called *Backyard Sugarin'* by Rink Mann, published by Countryman Press. It became my bible.

The process involves, to some extent, the same tools, methods, and accoutrements as making backyard whiskey, but unlike moonshine, you use what's left after the boil instead of distilling what comes off the boil. Also, chances are you won't get shot or do time for making maple syrup, that is unless you try to pass off some grade B as Grade A Medium Amber. Maple syrup fraud is, in Vermont, on the same heinous plane as cruelty to animals and treason.

As I found out, the best trees are the big, old road trees that can handle many taps and have the sweetest sap. There was certainly more than enough on my farm for a backyard operation. Each of the trees was capable of five or six taps each, the number of taps being determined by the circumference of the tree. One tap for every 10 inches, although it is better to under tap a tree than over tap if you really care about the health of the tree.

Even if you don't have this gold mine in your front yard, perhaps one of your neighbors who doesn't tap would let you borrow some of his trees in return for a pint or two. The rule of thumb is that you can expect to get about a pint of syrup per tap over the course of a season. For each gallon of syrup made you're going to need to harvest about 40 gallons of sap. My trees provided me with about 50 taps and so I figured I would produce somewhere in the neighborhood of five to six gallons. This is all rule of thumb and varies with each situation. Some sap is sweeter, some trees depending on southern exposure and weather conditions will produce more or less sap, and chances are with homemade equipment you'll run out of time and energy long before you've made all you can make. (I made about half what I could have, due to time constraints and third degree burns.)

For a backyard operation, one doesn't need thousands of dollars of sophisticated equipment, because there is no need for commercial efficiency, but you'd better be prepared to spend the best part of a day making a gallon of syrup on homemade equipment. Depending on the season you could end up boiling five or six times, which ends up being five or six days of nothing but standing around tending the operation. It's a great hobby, particularly if you're unemployed, or a writer.

A backyard operation can be put together very inexpensively and can pay for itself quickly if you make enough to give away the following Christmas. Nothing is better received down country when made with the giver's own hands.

There are few things you will need to start: a drill with a 7/16-inch bit, taps, buckets, a holding tank, an evaporator, a candy thermometer, filters and cans. This sounds like a very expensive list, but in reality it is not. Chances are you have a drill around the house. Taps cost 75 cents each and you'll not need many. Buckets can be recycled gallon milk jugs cut out to place under the taps. A couple of clean garbage cans make great holding tanks. An evaporator is fairly simple to construct if you're even the least bit capable, and filters and cans are inexpensive. A pint can costs $1.11 at Williams Store in Dorset, and that even includes the cap and the inner seal. If you're just making syrup for personal use, then mayonnaise jars will do just fine.

When to tap is always the big question. The optimum time is when the weather is warm and sunny during the day, and the temperature drops below freezing at night. I was always self-conscious though, not wanting to look stupid in front of all the natives by going out and tapping too early. I became a regular at Sherman's Store during the morning coffee hour. All the farmers came in around 8:00 to talk over coffee and doughnuts. I just waited till I heard them say they were going to tap and then I went out and started tapping as if I actually knew what I was doing.

When tapping the trees you need to drill a 7/16-inch hole at an slight upward slant just deep enough into the wood for the tap to go in up to the bucket hanger. You may have to knock off a little of the rough bark to get into the wood. You also want to tap underneath a large branch if possible because that's where the sap will flow the strongest. It will also flow stronger on the southern side of the tree, which will receive more sun.

You can use just about anything to hang under the spout to collect the sap. Recycled milk cartons are cheap and easy. Just cut a hole on the opposite side of the handle and hang it over the spout. Somehow, though, I couldn't see hanging milk cartons on those big road trees. I went looking for some old sap buckets and got them complete with lids from a local producer who had switched over to pipelines. There was something righteous about seeing buckets on those old trees and it looks much better in the photo album. This was the year Rupert had monumental windstorms during the spring. More than once I looked out the window and saw my buckets clattering toward town in the wind, thus finding myself chasing buckets and lids down Route 315.

Once the sap starts running it needs to be collected and put in the holding tank. A five-gallon sheetrock compound bucket is good for this chore, but beware, five gallons of sap is heavy if you have to haul it a great distance. I found putting the holding tanks on the back of my pickup and driving from tree to tree to be the best method; that is until I had to lift the 35-gallon can full of sap off the back of the truck. I just about had it on the ground when I fell and found myself awash in a sea of sap. From that point on, the holding tanks stayed on the tailgate.

When you first start, you'll think every drop of sap is precious and you will go to extraordinary lengths to avoid spilling it. Let me assure you that by the time the season is over, you will have sloshed and spilled an ocean of sap and you will still have more than you want. Nevertheless, when the garbage cans are full, then you have enough to begin your boil.

Obviously by now you have built yourself an evaporator. The better the evaporator the faster you're going to make syrup. There are many designs and I recommend you read the aforementioned book, but I'll describe what I did. I took a 55-gallon drum and turned it on its side. I took a Skil saw with a metal blade and cut a rectangular hole in the side about the size of the big flat pan I was going to use as an evaporator pan. The bigger the better. I then set the whole thing on concrete blocks so it was off the ground and at good working height. I cut a hole in the bottom of the barrel, which was now the back of the evaporator, and stuck in a stovepipe elbow, sealing the joint with stove cement. I ran the stovepipe flue up from there, supporting it with wire nailed to the eaves of the shed roof I was working in. I took the removable top (now the front) and cut a hole in it big enough to place an old flue damper I had lying around. Now when I loaded the barrel with wood for the fire, I could put the front back on and control the air by the use of this damper. This of course is easy to do when it's cold, but when that barrel is red hot and you're trying to take the front on and off to load wood, it can get pretty hot. More than a few times I near caught myself and everything around me on fire, and have the visible scars to prove it. Also be sure the flue is far enough away from the shed roof that it doesn't catch the whole thing on fire. You will find that sap is real handy for putting out small fires.

The evaporator worked fairly well, and I was able to keep the sap boiling, which is the most important thing. When the sap stops boiling, so does the process. The one thing you want to perfect is the art of continually adding sap to the boil without "killing the boil." I found the best way to do this was to set a large tin can on the corner of the evaporator pan filled with sap. I put a very small nail hole in the bottom edge so that a steady stream of sap would enter the boil but not enough to actually stop it from boiling. Then I adjusted the size of the hole to give me the largest stream I could get without stopping the boiling process. Half the fun of this whole project is figuring out ways to make it more efficient with home-made gadgets.

There are few do's and don'ts to boiling. You might think, well, instead of going to the trouble of building an evaporator, I'll just do it on the stove in a big pot. Before you do that, consider the fact that you are going to boil away about 40-plus gallons of water for every gallon of syrup. Imagine the result if someone brought a hose in the house and pumped 40 gallons of water around the room. Same result.

Boiling is an exceptional time for socializing. The weather brings your friends out, the fire is warm and guaranteed there is nowhere you can go till it's done. I had more than a few curious tourists stop and ask to take pictures as I was boiling. They would ask a bunch of questions, which I would laconically answer in my best Vermont accent as if I knew what I was doing. Little did they know they were taking snapshots of a born and bred southern boy who was boiling syrup for the first time in his life. As long as there's tons of sweet-smelling steam coming off your apparatus and obscuring everyone's vision, you'll look like you know what you're doing.

Long after your friends have left, the wife and kids have gone to bed, and the tourists are back downcountry, you will still be standing there boiling. The warm sun will have long since vanished, and you will be alternately freezing and roasting depending on your proximity to the evaporator. There finally comes a time when you say enough is enough. Chances are it's well past midnight. At that point you can take what you have in the pan that is almost syrup, and finish it in the house in a big pot on the stove. Even there, the sap will boil for what seems like an eternity and then suddenly the temperature will shoot upward and a layer of tiny bubbles will cover the surface of the syrup. When it reaches seven degrees above the boiling point of water, it's syrup.

 Keep in mind that the boiling point of water varies with altitude and barometric pressure, so it isn't always 212 degrees. Stick your thermometer in boiling water and calibrate it. If it's 213 degrees then you'll have syrup at 220 degrees. Anyway, if you aren't watching it, it can quickly turn to the equivalent of molten rock, which is just what it will be when it cools. I recommend not using your wife's expensive cookware, because if you screw up and let it go past, that pot is toast.

When it's syrup and still hot, run it through the wool filter cone into the can or jar and seal it while it's still hot. The filter removes a disgusting black substance called "niter" that is present in the sap and left by the boil in concentrated form.

There aren't too many things more satisfying than having your own personal stash of maple syrup in the pantry, particularly when you are the one that made it. It's a very impressive item when the foliage houseguests arrive. You also can feel real smug when wrapping a pint to send to your former business associates who are still toiling in the city. They just didn't think you had it in you. But best of all, you've taken one of nature's greatest gifts and through your own ingenuity and hard work have produced that which most people can only buy.

A Few Observations about Chickens

"How's that gator taste?"

"Great."

"What's it taste like?"

"Chicken. How 'bout that rattlesnake?"

"It's real tasty."

"What's it taste like?"

"Chicken."

Darwin may or may not have been correct in saying that man is descended from the apes, but I firmly believe that there are a host of animals in this world descended from the chicken. It occurred to me one day that I could open up an exotic foods restaurant, put a bunch of wild items on the menu and just make 'em out of chicken. Probably get away with it for a while as most people have not had the opportunity to eat snakes, gators and the like, but with a bit of fancy seasoning, they would just take your word for it. But that would be dishonest in the first place and in the second place, I did my time with chickens. During my agricultural period, I tried everything at least once and chickens were no exception.

As part of our journey back to simpler times, Mimi and I decided to have chickens to get fresh eggs every morning. We ordered 50 chicks from the local feed store, bought some equipment and went into the chicken and egg business.

If you think children are time-consuming, try raising 50 chicks to adolescence. Look at 'em cross-eyed and they die from fright. Too warm, they die. Too cold, they die. Essentially you are in charge of a chicken intensive care ward for about three months. To our credit, we never lost one, except for the one MacDuff the 150-pound Newfoundland stepped on in his zeal to become a mother hen.

First order of business was to build a chicken house. I started one morning and by the afternoon was pretty well on the way when a truck pulled up. Two of the town fathers stepped out and leaned against the truck as I was putting the roof on the house.

"Right nice building you got theah. What's it foah?"

"Chicken house." I wondered where this was going.

"Got a puhmit?"

"To build a chicken house?"

"Yup."

"Well, I didn't know I need a permit to build a chicken house. This is a farm and I just want a place to put my chickens."

"Need a puhmit from the zonin' boahd."

You got to be kiddin' me, I thought.

"Okay, where do I go to see the zoning board?"

"Me and Jaspah heah are the zonin' boahd."

Standing next to my already near complete chicken house, I asked, "Any chance I can build a chicken house?"

"Yup."

With that they got back in the truck and drove away. Too bad the Federal government doesn't work that way.

We raised the chickens and for a year had plenty of eggs. In fact, we were overrun with eggs. We sold eggs, gave away eggs, played egg toss with the kids, ate eggs for breakfast, lunch and dinner, but between the fresh bacon from old Lunch and Dinner (see the next chapter), fresh eggs and maple syrup, we were extremely pleased with ourselves, though we did notice we now couldn't button the top button on the side of our overalls.

At the end of a year, chickens quit laying and molt. Then it's time to get new chickens. So what do you do with the old ones? You slaughter them for the pot, of course.

Mimi was gone for the day and I decided to take care of it. The procedure was to humanely dispatch the hen (I will spare you those details, but there is some truth to "running around like a chicken with its head cut off") drop her briefly in a pot of boiling water to loosen her feathers and then pluck and clean. I think the book in which I read this was talking about doing one chicken. I'm not sure this was meant to do 50.

About five in the afternoon I took a break and was in the bathroom when I heard a scream. Mimi stood in the door of the kitchen staring at a blizzard of chicken feathers whirling around a bloody table of chicken guts, rounded out by a soaking wet floor from dunking dead chickens in the scalding pot. On one table lay about 40-plus scrawny, bony old chickens whose combined meat might make a couple of pounds of chicken salad. Chicken feathers drifted aimlessly through the house for weeks. Needless to say I slept alone for few days.

As it turns out, chickens that are good for laying eggs put all their energy into laying eggs and very little energy into getting fat. All those nice plump chickens walking around the yard were anorexic laying machines hiding under a clever disguise of plumage and feathers. Sort of like runway models actually. If you want eatin' chickens, you raise hens designed to get fat, who could not care one whit about reproduction. Essentially eatin' chickens are genetically "Reubenesque."

I did like the rooster though. While not necessary to the process of getting eggs to eat, what good is a farm with no rooster? There's something very rural and pleasing about hearing a rooster crow in the morning. As it turns out, our rooster became best friends with the horse. Sharing the henhouse with 50 women was a bit more than he could handle and he moved in with old Wally. They kind of reminded me of two old bachelors who spent their days hunting and fishing and their evenings throwing back gin and tonics with no one to answer to. On cold winter mornings when I walked in the barn, Studly Doright, as he was affectionately known, could be found perched comfortably on top of old Wally, staying nice and warm as old Wally was a thousand-pound heat generator. Unfortunately they must have had a falling out, or one too many gin and tonics, as one day I walked in to find old Wally calmly standing on top of poor Studly who was flatter than a roadkill chipmunk. Not much left except some reasonably good fly-tying material.

Truth is, I liked having chickens. A country home needs a chicken or two wandering around the yard. One of these days, when life slows a bit, the kids are gone and Orvis tires of having me around, I'm going to get me a few more chickens and a rooster too. Be nice to think that life could ever be simple enough again to replace the digital-projection-progressive-volume alarm clock with old Studly Doright II.

Hogs and Harmony

I was in the old chest freezer the other day looking for some ice cream. When I opened it, I saw nothing but glossy labels and marketing messages, from Stouffer's to Jimmy Dean sausage. What I didn't see was any plain white paper. Used to be this old freezer was fully stocked for the winter, everything was wrapped in plain white paper and hand labeled. If you're not following this train of thought yet, it used to be this old freezer was full of pork, beef, chicken and vegetables, all of which we raised ourselves. Now the only thing we raise is the lid on the freezer.

Mimi and I had our back-to-the-land phase. It lasted for a number of years and in fact ended up with 130 cows and a 200-acre dairy farm, but it first manifested itself in a desire to raise some pigs from spring through the fall and have fresh bacon and sausage all winter. New to Vermont, I had discovered the joys of real maple syrup and that Aunt Jemima and Mrs. Butterworth were both feckless imposters. All those years at the Waffle House wasted. Pancakes had become an obsession and the thought of home-raised bacon on the side was too much to resist.

We were working at Stratton at the time and we had access to all the kitchen garbage or free pig food, depending on how you viewed it. I built a small pen in April, bought two little pigs and we were in the pig-raising business. They were cute, but knowing full well their purpose, we named them Lunch and Dinner so as not to get too attached. Lunch and Dinner thrived on continental cuisine and soon they were big—very big. The pen looked smaller and smaller and the day came when I felt bad for them.

"Honey, I'm gonna let the pigs out for a walk." Mimi looked at me as if I had suddenly refused a piece of fried chicken.

"Are you out of your mind? Do not let those pigs out of that pen."

"I'm just going to let 'em walk around a bit."

"You are absolutely nuts if you open that gate."

"Where can they possibly go?" I asked.

"Look around. We're surrounded by a couple of million acres of national forest."

Something told me she was right, but a soft heart and total lack of common sense took over.

"It'll be fine. They're too fat to go anywhere."

Mimi walked into the house shaking her head. Something she seems to do a lot. In the back of my mind there was the nagging vision of the divorce papers. "Irreconcilable differences over hog rearing. Party of the first part heretofore known as wife is suing to force custody of pigs on party of the second part heretofore known as the idiot."

I opened the gate and Lunch and Dinner stepped out. At first they nosed around, exploring their surroundings. No problem, I thought. Then they began to move toward the road at an ever-increasing rate of speed. I ran to cut them off and was instantly educated to the speed and quickness of a thrill-seeking Duroc hog. Obviously fat is not an impediment to mobility in hogs.

"MIMI!" I yelled as loud as I could as I sprinted by the house in pursuit of the galloping pork.

"GET THE TRUCK!" The pigs were fast gaining separation as they headed down the dirt road toward the vastness of the national forest. Mimi blew by me, exhaust and expletives spewing from the truck, missing me by inches in an obvious demonstration of displeasure. She passed the galloping hogs and spun that truck around in a cloud of dirt and gravel to face the onrushing porkers. Damn, it was a thing of beauty and I fell in love all over again. Like a cowgirl (or hoggirl as it were) on a cuttin' horse she wheeled that old truck back and forth in front of those hogs until she turned them and headed them back home. As she passed, I reached for the door handle, but she would have none of it. No rides for the idiot who opened the gate.

Once back in the yard, Mimi and I ran back and forth with 2x4s for an hour driving Lunch and Dinner inexorably back toward the pen. No football game in my 20-year career taxed me more than maneuvering 400 pounds of suddenly emancipated pork back to prison. A bucket of grain and high-class restaurant slop finally enticed them back into the confines of their home. Unfortunately Mimi still had the 2x4 in her hand.

The next time Lunch and Dinner tasted momentary freedom was when they galloped up the ramp to the waiting truck. It was a sad moment and for a while I missed them terribly as they always greeted me with grunts of recognition and anticipation when I hauled the bucket of veal marsala, bananas foster, clams posilipo, frutti de mare and other culinary delights to their trough. That feeling of loss lasted right up until the time they reappeared as ribs, bacon and sausage. The smell of home-raised bacon frying on a crisp autumn morning dispelled any remaining sense of loss. By that time Mimi had somewhat forgiven me for the great hog roundup and my days of penance and humiliation were finally over.

I smiled, reached for my ice cream and took one last look at the Madison Avenue contents of the freezer. It reminded me we make choices in life. As much as I want to go back to farming, the freedom to follow my children across the playing fields of New England is too great to switch back to that adventurous, yet monastic life. I will be content for the present with normality. Not quite as much fun, but my children are the greater of two goods. Even so, I sure do miss ol' Lunch and Dinner.

Vermont Living

'Tis the Season

I am a self-confessed Christmas junkie. Even my kids don't like Christmas as much as I do. At least not until the big day when they fight over the loot. Myself, I start planning for the yuletide in September, which is about when the Ben Franklin in Manchester puts out their Christmas stuff. Some may think this behaviour a bit childish for a 6-foot-5, 280-pound ex-tackle. Perhaps. But I honestly don't think there's anybody alive today that's man enough to take away my *Bing Crosby Christmas Album*.

My deep southern upbringing is something that stirs my soul, but there came a time in life when I had to make a decision. As much as I love the south, celebrating Christmas down there takes too much imagination.

For one imbued with an overdose of yule yearning, sitting around in Bermudas, drinking a few cold Buds and watching *White Christmas* was terribly unfulfilling. Mall Santas, sweating profusely in polyester leisure Santa suits, and roasting chestnuts on the hot asphalt, just weren't doing the trick for this boy. I knew the time had come to move when I finished my last spray can of fake snow and I was only half done with the windows of the doublewide. At that very moment the local radio station played a selection from the *Johnny Paycheck Christmas Collection*. It was time for Vermont.

Why Vermont? This, my friends, is the mountaintop, the cathedral of Christmas. This is where Bing, Danny, Rosemary, and Mitzi saved the General and created the modern Yule legend. It's not hard to find book after book about Christmas in Vermont, but I don't recall ever seeing any beautiful coffee table books entitled *Christmas in Southeast Mississippi*. Vermont is also where they make those great beer commercials with the one-horse sleigh trotting through the snow to the strains of "I'll Be Home for Christmas." That one gets me all misty. I mean, here's a commercial that has so much Christmas spirit, it doesn't even mention the product till right there at the end, when they slap the name of the beer across the wreath on the front door. If Currier and Ives were alive today, they'd deem this area a target-rich environment.

Over the years here, my search for the true Christmas has sometimes eluded me, but anticipation of the event as in other things generally exceeds the event itself. On schedule I begin getting nervous about the first couple of weeks in September when the wind has its first little bite to it, and the *Sears Wish Book* arrives. Although Mimi loves Christmas too, she looks at me and shakes her head when I start whistling "Winter Wonderland" during foliage. Come Thanksgiving, the Fersen Christmas machine swings into high gear. Nothing gets me in the spirit more than the smell of Christmas cookies in the oven. Not to mention the fact that I am prone to eat three or four dozen at a sitting. A sure sign to the kids that the Christmas season is upon us is when Daddy walks in, flips on the *Time-Life Treasury of Christmas* album, cranks the volume to rock concert levels, drops that 100-pound sack of flour in the middle of the floor, and yells, "Alright!! Let's make some cookies!!"

One of the tougher aspects of Christmas is the perfect tree. The first prerequisite for a true country Christmas is hiking out into the snow-covered forest and cutting down your own Christmas tree. This invokes those wonderful scenes of families with sleds pulling large evergreens along a trail back to the house. Of course you must first be sure that you are cutting a tree off your own property or have permission to do so from the landowner. What Messrs. Currier and Ives never did show were those happy families sprinting for the sleigh under a hail of musket fire from the irate landowner. The other thing that's not evident in their paintings is the kids complaining that they are hungry, cold, how much farther, I gotta go number two real bad, and are there any malls in the Merck Forest. This all culminates when the eight-year-old whacks the five-year-old with a large iceball. It's about this time, in the interest of avoiding a prison term, I hand the axe to my wife.

Every year our December issue of *Country Living* arrives and we are automatically compelled to try to duplicate the front cover in our living room. What they don't tell you in *Country Living* is that Mother Nature doesn't grow those perfect trees you see on the cover. All those perfect trees are grown in nurseries and are trimmed each year by large guys with machetes whose job it is to make all the trees look like they belong on the cover of home decorating magazines. Mother Nature does not do this. She simply scatters a bunch of trees hither and yon, and you can go pick out what she has to offer. The first year on our farm, we hiked around our 60 acres until we discovered that we didn't have any evergreens on the place. So we did the next best thing. We hiked into the adjoining forest (with permission) in search of the perfect tree. The tree was finally chosen. It wasn't perfect by *Country Home*, *Redbook* or even *Biker Babes* standards but otherwise I thought it was a good tree.

"It's too tall."

"No way."

"Dear, it's too tall."

"Trust me babe, it's perfect."

Wanting to do this properly, I of course carried an axe to do the job. This looks great in the snapshots Mimi was taking, but is not terribly practical when trying to cut down a Christmas tree. In the first place there are branches all the way to the ground so there's no place to chop. So with Mimi holding the branches up and me crouched down in the fetal position next to the tree I began to hack away at the trunk. Not exactly the "Paul Bunyanesque" image I envisioned. I doubt he cut down any trees with his butt in the air. Nevertheless the tree was cut and we headed home with our prize. I proudly dragged the tree in through the front door, only doing minor damage to the door moldings, and took it to the corner where it was to stand. Of course it was too tall. By about two feet.

"Babe, I'll just trim it."

I ran down to the shop where all my chainsaws were kept. One of the romantic visions I had when moving to the country was heating with the wood from my own land. Think how inviting the smell of woodsmoke and the warmth of the woodstove are. And think of the economics. No longer would I have to pay those outrageous oil bills. I simply bought a $10,000 four-wheel-drive truck that gets about two miles to the gallon to haul the wood, and about $3,000 worth of chainsaws plus other assorted accessories for every woodland occasion and I was ready to live off the land. It was one of these assorted chainsaws that I brought back to trim the tree.

I guess Mimi assumed that I was going to take the tree back outside to trim it, because when I cranked up the chainsaw in the living room, she came screaming out of the kitchen yelling something about "nuts" that I really couldn't make out over the noise of the saw. Amazing how loud those things are in the house. I sort of hoped she was talking about whether I wanted nuts in the Christmas cookies.

WOOOOB WOB WOB WOOOB

"Just take a second, babe," I yelled over my shoulder.

I propped the tree up on the chair, eyeballed a measurement and kicked the old Stihl 041 into high mog. WOB WOOOOOOOOOOOOOOB I must admit that by the time I was finished there was an excessive amount of blue smoke floating around the house. Unfortunately we couldn't open the windows because of all the recently applied shrink-to-fit plastic. I also forgot about the automatic chain oiler. While I was warming her up and eyeballing the cut, I had the tip of the saw aimed at the wall. A little paint touchup and that big ol' oil stain just disappeared. I did have some trouble getting all the sawdust and woodchips out of the coffee table arrangement though, 'cause when I turned on the shop-vac it damn near sucked all the leaves off the poinsettias.

Once the tree was up we turned it about ten different ways, but couldn't seem to find a real good side. Each way we turned it there was a big hole that no amount of gaudy ornaments and tinsel was going to cover.

"No problem."

I took the section of tree I had cut off and trimmed off all the branches (this time I took it outside). I then returned my saw and came back with my drill and a spool of green picture wire.

"What are you doing?"

"Piece of cake, babe." I drilled holes in the trunk and then got out my Barlow and whittled the butt ends of the those branches into sharp points. By simply inserting those branches into the holes I was able to construct a magnificent Christmas tree. The picture wire supported the new branches by tying them to the branches above, thus enabling them to withstand the weight of the three thousand assorted ornaments and memorabilia that bedeck the Fersen Christmas monument. We now had a tree that would be the envy of any magazine art director.

Fragrance is a very important part of Christmas that is often overlooked by rookie aficionados. To achieve total Christmas, along with the ever present smell of cookies, you must interweave the essence of balsam evergreen.

This is pretty much impossible to do naturally unless you bring the chipper-shredder into the kitchen and run a few balsam fir saplings through it. Basically an old, incontinent Labrador will wipe out any natural balsam essence that one would get from the tree or the wreath. The answer is to buy naturally concentrated evergreen essence that is released by the means of heat. It comes with a hollow ring that fits over a lightbulb. You put one drop in the ring and the heat from the lightbulb sends out the smell of balsam fir. The trick is not to overdo it so that the guests at the annual Christmas cocktail soirée think it's natural. The other trick is to keep the Lab in the basement.

From the way I've been talking, one would think that there's nothing about the Christmas season that I don't like. But there are a couple. One is fruitcake. There was always fruitcake at Grandma Moon's house at Christmas. As far as I can discern it was always the same one. I don't ever remember seeing anybody eat any of it, and since they are impervious to rot, decay, and armor-piercing shellfire, I have to assume that it was the same one. I have been told that in our family there are heirloom fruitcakes that are sent back and forth every year between distant cousins and have been handed down for generations, thus perpetually solving the problem of what to do for Aunt Minnie Merle's side of the family.

The only other thing I can think of is Osmond Family Christmas specials. These guys are enough to make even good ol' Saint Nick mutter the word "dork" under his breath. Any network executive that allows this to go on the air should be sentenced to a South Georgia chain gang and forced to break fruitcakes in the hot sun.

Ménage à Truck
Me, My Wife, and a Big Red Dodge

Barring oxygen and chocolate ice cream, about the only thing in life I can't do without is a pickup truck. What other vehicle can haul a load of cow manure to your garden, be hosed out, and take you and your wife to dinner at the Barrows House that evening? Not something I'd want to try in a Volvo.

Pickups are a symbol of sorts, having replaced the horse in our collective American cowboy consciousness, and giving us that feeling of self-sufficiency as if there is no task we cannot perform as long as we've got us a truck. We can hunt, fish, and haul wood, building materials, livestock, you name it. To even attempt any of these pursuits with one of those big station wagons with wood on the side invokes visions of guys whose idea of roughing it is putting on blue jeans with creases pressed in, and wearing zip up demi-boots.

Basically owning a pickup comes down to that universal testosterone rush one gets from climbing into a big three-quarter-ton 4x4. It doesn't matter whether you're heading for deer camp in the Northeast Kingdom, or taking the wife to the local lawn and garden center to pick up some shrubs and a bag of peat moss. The fact is, if you've got you a truck, you are beholden to no one. Come Saturday morning you can put on those faded Levis, climb into that big cab, push in your George Jones tape that your wife won't let you play in the house, put a pinch between your cheek and gum, drop the kids off at the mall, and by God go down there and get them shrubs yourself. It's the closest I'll probably ever get to my secret dream of climbing into a Peterbilt with a big lighted Confederate flag across the grill, and heading down the interstate, drinking rocket fuel coffee and listening to that big diesel hum; the hiss of those air brakes and the sound of a set of dual, finely tuned, harmonizing air horns that play "Dixie"; the feel of that leather-wrapped wheel in one hand and that CB mike in the other. "HOW 'BOUT YA! YOU GOT THE ONE, BIG BUCKO, GO AHEAD!" Whew! Excuse me, I do get carried away.

A truck's versatility is unlimited and I bought my first when I was a junior in college. Pickups are wildly popular these days, but back then they weren't. The only people that drove pickups then were farmers and washing machine repairmen. My reason for buying one was twofold. I'm 6-foot-5, and trying to park in the back seat of a Plymouth was impossible. A pickup seemed to be the answer. Talk about room to maneuver. Also, my old '62 Plymouth Fury convertible failed inspection on fourteen counts, and it was either jail time or a new vehicle. I bought a brand new Ford pickup. At that time, all the girls were driving pastel Cutlass convertibles, and all the guys were driving Malibu SS 396s, so it was a bit of a novelty when I drove in with my first truck. As it turned out, it became the most utilized vehicle at the jock dorm. It was the only vehicle that could accommodate the entire offensive line on our daily forays through campus. Since most of us never went to class, we would sit around and play poker all day until football practice. Then every hour, on the hour, we'd all pile in the truck.

"Big R" and I would ride up front, with "Pork Hawg," "The Duck," "Big Chat," "Jelly Belly" and "Burly Bob Honeycutt" in the back. We'd drive around campus during class change, expressing our admiration for the attributes of the lovely co-eds, and then it was back to "Weasel" and "Skyscraper's" room for another hour of walking cane and seven stud, shuck, roll back.

Two years later after being drafted into the NFL, I dabbled briefly with an Electra 225 Sport Coupe, but found it severely limiting. It was great for impressing women, but absolutely useless for hunting and fishing. So I bought me another truck.

This time it was a GMC Sierra with a 454 Invader engine. It had an AM-FM stereo eight track with a built in CB and loudspeaker system. This is a great item for singing a little country music with a few friends in "Swine-O's" parking lot at about four in the morning, not to mention riding around all the old parking spots, pulling up behind a car, turning on the brights, and then flipping on the loudspeaker. "I HOPE Y'ALL AIN'T NEKID IN THERE!!" But then I was too mature to do stuff like that.

I installed high-performance glasspacks and headers, which gave it the resonance of an old Chris Craft and with that 454 engine, it had the ability to blow the doors off most anything around. It was during this time that I spent a brief period in training camp with the New York Giants. I decided one day to visit the city and do some sightseeing, so I rumbled on down the Sawmill Parkway into the city where I promptly got lost. After an hour or so of wandering around, I began to notice a lot of people staring at me and my truck. As it turned out, I was rumbling through Harlem in a pickup truck with a gun rack (fortunately empty) and Georgia license plates. I managed to survive that, and a year later a brief, unsuccessful marriage, due in part to the fact that she wouldn't let me keep my truck. I ended up having to drive a Volkswagen Rabbit. Enough said.

The Dodge came into my life when I moved here to Vermont. There are only two things I can point to that have been with me since my early days in Vermont some fourteen years ago. One is my wife, the other is this truck. They came into my life about the same time and happily, they're both still running. I consider that impressive when you consider the national marriage statistics and the life expectancy of a 4x4 pickup in Vermont.

There comes a point in a truck's life when it is either too big a piece of junk to trade in, or there is too much sentimental value placed on it to ever consider getting rid of it. That point also comes in a marriage. I'm not quite sure in which category Mimi has me placed at this point, but in the case of my Dodge Power Wagon, it is both. Eventually it will end up as a treasured lawn sculpture.

It was with us when we bought the farm in Rupert and our "back to the land" vision went into overload. We started with two beef cows and some chickens in 1982, and wound up with 130-plus dairy cows and heifers in New York by 1991. It has 100,000 miles on it, all of which were put on it in pastures, down logging roads, in the woods, hauling cattle, fertilizer, wood, whatever was needed. It pulled tractors out of the mud, chased heifers through plowed fields spewing roostertails of mud, and towed more than a few loaded hay and forage wagons.

There was the time Mimi and I were hauling some heifers back from Northern Vermont. I'd built a rack for the back of the truck, but being fairly new to this, had built it wrong. About halfway back it began to disintegrate and we were stopping every couple of miles to try and patch it together, meanwhile keeping those by now crazed heifers from jumping out of the truck.

"Dear, what's that hissing sound?" I dodged a flailing hoof just in time to hear the sound of air escaping from a tire. Fortunately it was coming from the valve stem. Unfortunatly, the spare had been taken out to accommodate the cattle and there was only a little store across the road.

"Quick! Get over there and buy some bubble gum!" When she got back, we both started chewing like hell until we had enough to pack around the leak. By the time we got home, the truck was listing about ten degrees to starboard. In the back were the shattered remnants of my rack and two slightly panic-stricken heifers, who, judging by the ambiance in the back of the truck, gave new meaning to the phrase "scared s___less."

The most recent indignity suffered by this old truck was being driven into a ravine by a dog. I had just walked back in the house to get something I forgot. Yoo Hoo, my Lab, was in the truck as always, and the engine was running. When I walked back out the truck was gone.

"MIMI!! SOMEBODY STOLE THE TRUCK!!" I yelled as I sprinted down the driveway. There had been a light snow the night before and the tracks were clear in the driveway and suddenly I noticed the track veered perfectly between two large oaks and over the edge of the ravine. I dashed over, and there at the bottom sat the truck resting comfortably on a log amidst the alders and the dead swamp grass. When I got to the door and pulled it open, Yoo Hoo was sitting with his paws on the steering wheel, wagging his tail furiously. It seems he had jumped up on the wheel and knocked the shift lever into drive. Of course in the excitement of the ride he had whizzed all over the front seat. By that time Mimi had arrived at the top of the driveway.

"It's all right, dear," I yelled, "Yoo Hoo just drove the truck over a cliff." I looked up to see her walking away shaking her head and slapping herself on the forehead. The problem now was how to get the truck out of the ravine. The easy answer would be to call a tow truck and have them pull it out. But being a proud individual, I wasn't looking forward to explaining to the grinning tow truck operator that my dog had driven my truck over a cliff. Particularly a dog named Yoo Hoo.

I own a tractor and a Jeep. I drove the tractor down into the ravine and pulled the truck off the log it was resting on. I got it into a good enough position where I could take a run at backing it up onto the road. The problem was I had to back it full speed up a frozen slope between the two major oak trees that Yoo Hoo had managed to drive between. I put it in four-wheel, low lock, popped it into reverse, took a quick look back and gunned it back up the bank, slinging frozen mud and rocks and ripping off the side mirror on the oak tree. I got it far enough to where the Jeep could pull it the rest of the way and it was out.

Now all that was left was to get the tractor out, but because of the frozen mud, it just kept sliding back in. The only other way out was by taking a less direct and flatter route through the woods using the tractor as a sort of mini-bulldozer to knock over the saplings and bushes in its path. This resulted in the creation of a rather lovely nature trail near my house.

The truck has earned itself a place in semi-retirement. Its last great effort was to help us build our house here in Dorset, hauling building materials. Now it's used only occasionally as a spare mode of transportation, but is still considered the most reliable vehicle in the driveway. It runs fairly well if the temperature is somewhere in the high seventies. Anything lower and the warmup time, so that it will actually move, goes up in direct proportion to the drop in temperature. In the dead of winter, any use of the truck requires considerable advanced planning.

The body is beginning to have its problems. The side panels are now the consistency of saltines, and when I took it to the carwash the other day, the pressure washer blew a hole in the side. There's also a fairly large hole in the floorboard, giving one the impression of what it must be like to drive Fred Flintstone's car.

It would be easy here to get maudlin over this truck, but it is, after all, a piece of machinery. What this truck does have, though, is that which can't be purchased. It has patina. That intangible gift that only time can give a fine antique or a good pair of blue jeans. In the case of this truck, it manifests itself in dented grills, broken lights and missing tailgate. When the mirror falls off on hitting a bump, it adds to the patina factor. It has survived to that stage where every new ding adds luster and it passes inspection through the gracious imagination of the mechanic. Conversation is impossible at speeds above 30 miles per hour because of wind noise through the door. But all this has given it a certain "road warrior" invincibility. It's like that guy in the bar that you know better than to mess with.

He's so screwed up he has nothing to lose. That same aura emanates from this truck. One has only to drive it into Manchester on a busy day and notice the German imports scattering and yielding the right of way at every turn. This old truck ain't got nothing to lose.

Extreme Gardening

One of the first things that people do when they move to Vermont is start a vegetable garden. It seems to be a of rite of passage that if you're going to live here in the country, then it's incumbent upon you to produce your own food. You can just hear the phone conversation.

"Mona, you wouldn't believe how wonderful it is up here. We've even started a garden to grow our own vegetables. Marty is down at the lawn and garden now buying a rototiller. We've become real Vermonters."

Of course ol' Marty is yet to dip that rototiller into Vermont soil, which is like dropping a spoon down a disposal. All that steel on rock makes one hell of a racket. I know this for a fact because I was, and still am, as guilty as poor ol' Marty; the only difference is I have 15 years of hardened experience as a Vermont rock gardener, and I've learned a few things.

My first garden here was a plot shared with my buddy Doug Clark. We rented a piece of junk, front-tine tiller and proceeded to try to till up what would pass for a good granite quarry. I knew I was in trouble when I showed up with a shovel and hoe and Doug came out

of the house with crowbars, pikes and a county exten-
sion bulletin, which I believe was titled *Dynamite and
Its Uses in the Small Vegetable Garden.*

As a result of that experience, one of the first purchases
I made when I decided to stay here was a rototiller. Not
just any rototiller, but the Troy-Bilt Horse Model 8-Hp
Professional. The top of the line, head-honcho model of
the biggest and best tiller company in the world. This
is the tiller that could clean up Vermont, as it has the
capability of turning under and composting just about
anything including rusted-out junk cars. With this hawg
in hand I was ready for anything Mother Vermont could
serve up in the rock department. Fourteen years and
a few thousand rocks later, that faded old tiller is still
churning up stones.

I grew up around gardens, toddling behind my
Grandma Moon on those sultry afternoons in south
Georgia. We didn't have any rocks, but we did have
locusts. She seemed to be constantly on locust patrol
looking for these giant black locusts that you could hear
munching if you were quiet enough. As a little boy they
scared me to death, but I used to love to watch Grandma
as she grabbed them up off her vegetables and ripped
their heads off, leaving them thrashing in the red dust.
The corpse-littered walkways served as a warning to the
others to stay the hell out of Miz Moon's garden—so I
guess I came by my desire to plant vegetable gardens
honestly, because every year when the snow melts and
the days get warm I'm out there getting my garden ready.
The only trouble is that this ain't south Georgia, this is
Vermont, a place where Sisyphus, if offered the choice

of gardening or pushing the boulder up the mountain, would probably choose the boulder.

There are three distinct phases in the Vermont growing season. There's the early enthusiastic "let's get out there and till that soil!" season, the middle, or "damn, look at all those weeds!" season, and the late "you think there's anything under all that mess?" season. The more you garden in Vermont the shorter the first season becomes and the longer the later seasons become.

One of the first lessons I learned is that up here, basically you can grow corn and beans, which are fine, and all that cold weather stuff like kale and brussels sprouts, which ain't so fine. You can grow tomatoes if you start 'em inside about Christmas. Always be sure to start twice as many as you want to grow because the minute you put 'em outside you can hear 'em screaming "NO! NO! Not out here!" and half of 'em die of fright.

You can also grow giant man-eating zucchinis that are absolutely tasteless, but the staple of every Vermont garden. I finally discovered why so many people grow zucchini up here. As it turns out, giant zucchinis make great targets for sighting in your deer rifle. Nothing explodes quite as nicely as a 40-pound zucchini when hit by a hollow point 30-06.

What you can't grow up here are the absolute essentials of life like okra, butter beans, field peas, black-eyed peas and peaches. Now I'm sure some horticultural cabbage-head out there is going to write me a scathing letter telling me all about the things they've grown and how successful they've been gardening here in this agricultural paradise. Of course these are the trust funders that build massive cold frames and then sit next to them adjusting them every five minutes so that the ambient temperature stays at a constant 73.5 degrees. Any more or less and the plants immediately die. Trust me, I've tried with great unsuccess. Taking care of a garden is one thing, sleeping in the thing to share your body heat is another. This practice continues until the famous "all danger of frost is past" period, which in Vermont begins and ends on July 4th weekend.

One perpetual problem we have in our garden is Mimi won't let me thin it out enough. One of the cardinal rules of good gardening is to thin stuff out so it has room to grow. Year after year Mimi plants about six squash and zucchini plants per hill, which is supposed to be thinned to one. Whenever I get ready to thin the garden she yells that one might die and then we wouldn't have any of that superior, super-hybrid, tasteless zucchini. So we leave them and by the end of the season we're hacking through a rainforest of giant zucchini and squash plants trying to find the entrance to the house. Out of all this Mimi then makes the ceremonial and traditional one loaf of zucchini bread and the rest of the tonnage then lies there until the week before deer season.

Over the years our gardens have evolved from complex raised-bed affairs with a couple of hundred different species of succession plantings, and elaborate canning and root cellar facilities, to a big plot of green beans and zucchini. We till up the garden in the spring, plant a boxcar load of beans and zucchini and in the fall hack our way through the vines and harvest a couple of wheelbarrows of giant, tough, green beans, which we then consume in the next week so we don't have to process any of it. This has a lot to do with age, jobs and priorities. Our first gardens were actually vehicles of survival in a tough economic climate. Now that we have evolved to middle age with real jobs and children, the time and effort to do these things has vanished in a blur of soccer, lacrosse, T-ball games and work.

But there is still a reason each spring to get out there and stick our hands in the dirt, even if we know the result is going to be modest at best. It's one of our connections to our youthful past when we could get by on very little and our responsibilities were few. It was a time when we heated with wood out of necessity, when all our life's adventure lay in front of us. It's a reminder of why we came here in the first place—something that can easily get lost if you let it.

The Raising

A few months ago, we finished building a house. Although finished is a euphemism for stopped. What we actually did was stop building a house. I've discovered over the years that "home ownership" and "finished" are contradictory terms. I've lived in houses that were a couple of centuries old and far from finished.

I occasionally sense a kinship with whoever built those older homes, when I consider that his weekends were probably consumed by home improvement much as mine are. He was a craftsman, armed only with a few hand tools, puttering about the house with his list, scratched out by his wife in the flickering candlelight the night before. During the week it was back to hunting, fishing and ripping off the Indians under the Manifest Destiny clause. I, on the other hand, own a Craftsman, a Troy-Bilt, a Black and Decker, and a host of other handy-dandy home improvement items, total cost probably more than the house. My list for the weekend was discovered this morning, stuck to the toilet seat on a Post-it note.

Anyway, for the time being I've stopped building. As much as I've enjoyed this exercise in creativity, the six months I took off to build this house are over, and I must go back and get a "real" job, as if building my own house was a vacation.

During the course of construction, I would meet people at one soirée or another, and invariably they would ask me what I do. I had two choices. I could tell them I was a writer, or I could tell them I was building my own house. In either case there was always an awkward silence as they waited for me to tell them what I really did. After a while I stopped trying to explain and just let them assume that I was independently wealthy.

It's my job to put a roof over our heads, keep the family warm and fed. That's what I'm supposed to do. That's what men (yes, ladies, and now women) have been doing for the past million years.

Somewhere in the distant past, mankind discovered that of all the creatures he encountered, he was the least equipped to survive. Generally everything he ran into was either bigger, stronger, faster or had more hair than he did. In the worst case scenario, all four. He did however possess one superior weapon, and that was reason.

He certainly didn't understand it, but he seemed to be able to outsmart the other creatures, most of the time.

This reason led him to understand the need for shelter, both from the elements and from the beasts that were constantly enjoying him for lunch. At some point in our journey through life, man walked into a cave, drew some branches across the opening and ascertained that this worked pretty well. We had our first house. When he communicated this fact to others of his kind, they occupied the surrounding caves, and we had the first subdivision.

I've dug my first cave, if you will, pulled my family inside and drawn the branches across the front. It certainly isn't the first house I have lived in, but it is the first one I've built with my own hands; the first one to appear on the landscape as a function of my designs, as opposed to those of some other long dead architect. It was something that I've always wanted to do, but never had the money nor the courage to attempt. I simply kept buying older houses and fixing them up.

Not this time. I've been down the ol' "Honey let's buy an old farmhouse and fix it up" routine. I've crawled through the frozen mud of enough spider-infested crawl spaces to thaw out leaky old plumbing. I've repaired enough slimy rotted sill plates and replaced tons of soggy insulation. I've spent more than a few winters standing in front of warped windows with a hair dryer installing shrink-to-fit plastic. This time I wanted a house where everything worked at least for a little while. The time had come to build my own; to leave my footprint on this earth.

We decided to build a post-and-beam house. If Mimi couldn't have an old house, at least it was going to look old. Anyway there is something very reassuring about walking into a house where the frame is exposed and all one sees are massive beams of solid oak and pine. As a former fullback and friend of mine might muse between expectorations, "By God, ain't no wolf gonna huff and puff and blow this sumbitch down."

It doesn't sway or creak in the winter wind, and it's impervious to the depredations of five-year-olds (who, by the way, can easily knock B. B. Wolf into the nickel seats when it comes to destructive capability).

The walls are formed by 10-inch by 10-inch posts of red oak and the roof is held up by 5-inch by 7-inch rafters of white pine. There are no nails in this frame to work loose with age, only oaken pegs driven into the mortise and tenon joints that tighten as they shrink with age. In time, those pegs will be impossible to remove.

It's an art that was almost forgotten, but is making a big comeback these days, not only because of its strength and beauty, but because with the new technology, it has become the most energy-efficient way to build. Without getting terribly technical, the frame is surrounded by an envelope of insulation that makes the house as tight as one could hope. After living for years in houses where the curtains fluttered in the wind even with the window closed, and zone heating meant a zone within three feet of the woodstove, this has been a wonderful experience. I realize this doesn't conform to the true Vermont lifestyle scenario, but this business of 50-degree temperature swings in the house and sleeping in sweats becomes tiresome. I've paid those dues tenfold.

Possibly the best part of the experience was the chance to work with Ken and Tom, who we hired to help build the house. Tom handled the general contracting, Ken was the craftsman responsible for the post-and-beam frame, and I was the forklift. Whenever a 30-foot beam needed to be moved around, or a 200-pound panel held in place for nailing it was "Hey, somebody get Bucko." When it was time for some intricate finish work, I was immediately sent on a vital errand. Coming from the "hell, just eyeball it" school of carpentry, my finish skills were not highly in demand here.

A post-and-beam frame is laid out and created on the ground. The mortises and tenons are chiseled and cut, the beams are hewn and planed, peg holes drilled, and all preparations made for the frame to be raised all at once. There is something very gratifying about spending a day, bent over a 700-pound oak beam with a chisel and mallet in your hand, shaving, chipping, and tapping at this monster that you realize will eventually be the corner post of your home.

I was given the task of planing the beams before they were stacked in the finish pile. The plane in my hands was old, with a smooth, worn handle wrapped around a blade sharp enough with which to shave. In fact, there's more than a few bloodstains on these beams as a result of my "precision craftsmanship." There was no plastic, no cord dangling from the end, just wood and steel and human ligament for power. The plane slid along the beam surface, curling up a ribbon of wood so thin as to be transparent. Each stroke left the wood marble-smooth. Only the wind, the quiet rasping of the plane, and my occasional epithets and disgusting sucking noises from trying to stop the bleeding, broke the silence.

As the days stretched into weeks, the pile of rough cut, dimensional beams on one side of the barn shrank, and the pile of finished beams grew on the other side, each edge chamfered, each tenon tapered. By the end of the project, there was a mountain of chips, shavings and sawdust around the work area. In front of us was a massive pile of gleaming timbers, smooth as a baby's butt, each with curves, notches, and angles that created an imperceptible line between construction material and art.

The morning of the raising dawned cold and misty. Our friends and neighbors began to gather, the men and more than a few women headed for the work site, while Mimi and others began to prepare food around the bonfire we started to keep everyone warm. Children and dogs were everywhere; in the woods, out of the woods, in the creek, up in the trees. It was a spectacle of Amish proportions, only in lieu of the blues and blacks of the Amish were the reds, greens, and neons of L. L.Bean, CB, and Descente.

Because of the cold misting rain, there was some discussion as to whether to postpone or not, but the consensus was to continue. At nine o'clock, the first timbers were joined and pegged together and the process began. Each section of the house consisted of three posts supporting one huge 32-foot cross beam, each post braced diagonally on both sides. The diagonal braces were curved instead of straight to give the frame an elegant look. The 23 braces alone required three men and two weeks to complete by hand.

Each one of these sections easily weighed close to a ton and required between 15 and 20 people to lift into place. The sections were pegged together on the ground and then with two men at the base of each post to guide it into position, the count was given and the entire crew heaved the section upright with all the accompanying guttural utterances and grunting, which rose in crescendo until it slammed into place.

It was organized chaos at best, for the majority had no idea what they were doing, myself included. There were innkeepers, accountants, ski bums, a magazine publisher, a college professor, and a few Wall Street types mixed in with some farmers, and topped off with a trust-funder or two. At one point I watched a middle-aged Yale graduate of old-school breeding, in his tweed work clothes, holding up a floor joist with a tobacco chewing, deer poaching native who spat and cussed with the regularity of a metronome. Remarkably they were carrying on a rather animated conversation seasoned with gales of laughter. It would have been a tough group for Mrs. Vanderbilt to seat properly at a formal dinner, but tossing around a few tons of oak and pine is a great equalizer.

Fortunately under Ken's guidance, and with the help of some of his more knowledgeable friends, everyone was placed properly amid the laughter and the insults. For all the fun we were having, we were aware of the fact that there was a significant danger involved. One had only to wrap his arms around one of these beams to realize what would happen if you ended up underneath one of them.

By the time the rafters were being placed in position the sky was cloudless, and the fall colors were brilliant. At one point, I stood off to the side and watched the activity, the hustle, the muddy kids, the women laughing by the fire, occasionally yelling to a child who was getting too near the work site. The frame was towering above us some 30-plus feet, and the sun was heading toward the western hills. I realized there would be very few moments in life that surpassed this one. It was one of those rare occasions when life gathers its finest elements and lays them at your feet. I watched two-year-old Trevor Devries, splashing in a mud puddle to the delight of the other children and the palms-upward dismay of his mother. A young woman sat on a stump off to the side nursing a child. Groups of men, clinging in clusters to the frame, were laughing amidst the shouts directing the rafters into place. Above me a V-shaped wedge of Canadian geese honked their way south. The wind rustled the red maples around me, and if there was a way to freeze that moment, I would have done so. Perhaps it's best I couldn't. To examine something too closely is to risk finding flaw. This fleeting moment deserved better.

A shout from the roof signaled I was needed, probably to toss up a couple of 200-pound beams or something.

By five o'clock the frame was almost done. The last rafter fell into place with a roar of approval from the crowd below. There remained only the task of offering our thanks to the Druid gods who had provided the trees for this structure. My son Nicholas and I climbed into the crane bucket that we used to lift the rafters. With an evergreen branch in hand, we rose to the peak of the frame and attached the branch in homage. It was accomplished with mixed emotions: relief that it had come together so well, sadness that it was over, and rising panic at being suspended 60 feet in the air in a damn bucket. The frame was complete. Again a roar from the group below.

Darkness was coming soon. The sky was purple and the bonfire cracked and popped as our friends came to say their good-byes and congratulations. Exhausted children disappeared into the darkness on the shoulders of their parents. Soon there were only a few of us left around the embers. Ken, Tom and I sat with coffee in hand, saying very little and staring at the frame. There was exhaustion and elation, even a touch of sadness. The task of completing the house still lay before us, but what stood before us now was something special, a work that by its very nature and strength could endure for centuries. A footprint.

"Stuff"

"Stuff" is just another term for matter. You can't destroy stuff. You can jump up and down on it, let the dog sleep on it, store it in a damp basement, but it never goes away. What's more, even if you take it out and get rid of it, it comes back. Even the sacred tag sale ritual or Salvation Army trip will only be a temporary divestiture, as it will slowly creep back into your house.

There's a very good reason for this, which I've discovered after years of intensive research. I call it *Fersen's Law of Multiplying Material and Pack Rat Principle*. Mimi and I have owned four houses in ascending order of size and within three months of moving into each one, they have been slam-packed to the rafters, and the simple reason is, because you always walk into your house carrying something, and you always leave your house empty-handed. I believe it to be a natural law, relative to squirrels putting up nuts for the winter. Somehow or another we have evolved past the nut stage into the "whatever the hell we can get cheap whether we need it or not" stage. One only has to watch the cars screeching to a halt at tag sales or arriving hours, even the day, before it starts to buy "stuff." We don't necessarily need it, but we can't resist the opportunity to buy something if we think we're gonna save a dime. The other day Mimi came home from the Barrows House with a pagoda shaped, satin tufted headboard that would have done justice to any whorehouse in the country. I just looked in amazement and asked her, "What in the hell are we going to do with that?" Her reply was she thought we could saw off the ugly part on the top and have it re-covered. Of course all that would have cost about three times what a regular headboard would cost. Nonetheless, there it sits in the basement, the centerpiece to a stunning arrangement of junk, and "stuff."

One of the great events in Rupert, Vermont is the annual firemen's auction to raise money for the fire company. The premise here is that people in the village donate junk to the auction, and then go to the auction and buy everybody else's junk. In essence, everybody just trades junk and the fire company gets a fee for moving it around. Of course the following year, the same junk comes out of the basement or attic and is auctioned off again. I'm sure some of this crap has seen every attic in Rupert. What's interesting is to watch the tactics used to sell this stuff. These firemen aren't stupid. They know that a lot of this stuff is too crummy even for a real foaming-at-the-mouth pack rat to buy so they use the patented Bus Mars "throw in the junk with the good stuff" tactic. They get the occasional piece that they know people are going to bid on, and they put it in a box of garbage that nobody in their right mind would buy. By doing this they force the bidder to take the garbage and add it to his "stuff" collection.

Very shrewd. Even so, after the auction there's a couple of bucket-loader loads of junk to haul away and add to Mother Nature's "stuff" collection. But, since it's for the benefit of the fire company and everybody seems to enjoy it, there's no harm done. I myself have purchased a lovely Minnesota Vikings trash can and a pair of roller skates, although I had to buy a box full of used underwear to get the trash can.

Noah Webster defines "stuff" as: *the furnishings or chattel of a place or home*, and he defines "junk" as: *secondhand worn or discarded articles having little or no commercial value*. Anyway, "chattel" is a pretty interesting word. Used in a sentence you could say: "After the kids have been playing inside all day, it looks like there was a chattel stampede."

The problem is not so much with the kids, it's with the amount of junk and/or stuff we have in the house that has no place. Even I could keep a house clean when there's somewhere to put everything, and I've been compared more than once to our porcine brethren, but my house has achieved severe junk and stuff overload, and occasionally I find myself in one of those moods to eliminate anything from my life that has not been used in the past couple of days. Mimi gets in these moods as well, but for some reason they never seem to coincide. This sets the scene for the consummate battle of wits. Both of us go into super rationalization mode to try and defend our positions on why something should go away and why it should stay. Perhaps this is nature's way, because if one of these moods should strike us simultaneously, we would find ourselves standing buck naked in the wilderness, devoid of any possessions. I for one am appalled at the amount of Tupperware in our house. We just built a brand new house and spent the greatest portion of the money on the kitchen and now the cabinets are literally bursting with old Tupperware. Every time I open a cabinet or drawer to get something, about ten pieces of that plastic "stuff" hits the floor and I spend the great majority of my life picking up Tupperware and stuffing it back into overloaded cabinets. The maddening thing is it just sits there in the damn cabinets with most of the lids that don't fit any of the bottoms. One night I'm going to have to pull off a midnight Tupperware removal raid, but of course there is method in Mimi's madness 'cause she knows the minute I open those cabinets, the Tupperware avalanche will wake her up.

There are of course a few knickknacks of mine that have great import and are not to be touched. My T-shirt and old football jersey collection for one, many of which are well over 25 years old. The other day I walked in with four new Orvis T-shirts and Mimi just looked at me and said something to the effect that I already owned about 5,000 T-shirts, to which I replied, "I'll get rid of a T-shirt for every piece of Tupperware you get rid of." End of discussion.

The other things that are not to be touched are my college football helmet, my red and white flashing Budweiser sign, my football cleats, my life sized portrait of Nathan Bedford Forrest and anything that has to do with hunting, fishing or John Wayne. Oh yeah, and my children most of the time.

The children's contribution to this ever mounting mountain of material is monumental. The paper blizzard that comes home from their school is enough to heat the house for the winter, but since they are projects of great import, I am not wont to burn them, yet I find my office already buried in mounds of their projects, pictures and presents, and they're only in the second and fourth grades respectively.

I have started a secret project to try and eliminate some of the overload or at least maintain a balance of power between and man and material. Every day when I leave for work, I now take something out of the house and throw it away. Yesterday I took Elizabeth's chewed up Barbies. Once in a while Yoo Hoo (the famous truck driving dog) gets bored and chews up a few Barbie and Ken dolls. You would think Elizabeth would want to throw them away, but hell no, now they become the Shark Attack Barbie Playset in the bathtub. One-armed Ken bravely swims out to rescue footless and handless Barbie. So far Elizabeth hasn't missed them yet, but in a month or so I'm gonna have to make her take a bath.

To top all this off, my mother, bless her heart, passed away a few months ago. We were in the process of planning to build an addition on the house for her retirement years. After the funeral I figured that project was canceled, but what I found is that I'm going to have to build the addition anyway just to keep her stuff. I really didn't think she had much of anything important until after the funeral when my Aunt Ginny, Aunt Marianne and Aunt Kathy went through the house with me explaining what everything was and its historical significance to the family. As it turns out I am not going to be able to throw away, sell or burn anything.

"This was Aunt Kateola's [pronounced Kate-Ola] nut dish she got from Grandma Woolfolk for her fiftieth anniversary and it's a real treasure. Nicky and Elizabeth will want this when they get older."

As I listened to this, I watched Nicky chasing Elizabeth around the front yard with a big stick and thought to myself. "Yep, I'll bet Nicky just can't wait to get hold of Aunt Kateola's nut dish." But I love my aunts dearly and I'd never do anything to upset them, so it looks like I'm stuck with a whole bunch of Aunt Kateola nut dishes and a collection of lace doilies from Cousin Minnie Merle David's side of the family, not to mention mother's huge church organ. It took up one whole room in her house and now has to find a place in our house, which in the time it took you to read this has accumulated 275 more cubic feet of junk and/or "stuff."

There was one thing I found in the back recesses of her closet. A huge box, which when opened revealed every little project I had done for her as a child. Bookmarks, hand prints with poems, Valentine cards, she had them all. She had carried them around with her for some 30 years although her modest abodes had no room for such things. I took the box, carried it home, and placed it in my office with all the things my children had given me. There is no room for it, but it will stay along with whatever else my kids bring me. If need be I'll store it in some Tupperware.

The Rights of Spring

"Well, honey, whaddya think?"

"I don't know, dear, it looks pretty bad."

"Well, I'll go check it out."

I step out of my truck and walk down the road through a sea of mud to the edge of that fabled spot where even the road grader has buried itself numerous times and countless citizens have disappeared into the seething muck. It is the Scylla and Charybdis of Vermont dirt roads where one mistake, one slight hesitation, and you'll disappear forever, only to be dug up two or three thousand years from now, frozen in some Pompeiian-like pose still sitting in your car.

She leans her head out the window.

"How does it look?"

Looking back at Mimi, I'm standing in a rut that comes up above my waist. Mud and gravel ooze menacingly around me. It's alive and you can hear it gurgle and click as the water and stones slowly shift and move. I shiver and hurry back to the truck, climbing in and kicking off the clinging mud. In my best Marshall Dillon voice I reply.

"Looks pretty bad, Miss Mimi, but we got no choice. We have to get to town for supplies."

"But can we make it?"

John Wayne chimes in.

"Don't you worry your pretty head, little lady, I'm taking this rig through to Manchester."

I back the old red stagecoach up to the top of the knoll, kick her into four-wheel drive and, revving the engine to full power, pop it into drive and floor it.

"HANG ON, PILGRIM!! YEEEEEEEAAAAHHHHH!!"

The old red truck leaps forward, rusted sheet metal flapping in the wind. Mimi grabs the dashboard, her eyes the size of Franklin Mint commemorative plates. By the time we reach the edge of the abyss we're doing about 45 miles an hour. Momentarily the old girl dances lightly over the bubbling cauldron, but then the bottom drops out from under us, slamming us forward, as the hungry road sucks and drags on our struggling steed. The wheels spin violently, throwing up a chocolate roostertail of frothing mud, spitting rocks and gravel into the surrounding forest. You know every squirrel and chipmunk in the vicinity is diving for cover.

"COME ON BABY, YOU CAN DO IT! HEEEYAH!!!!"

I keep my foot jammed to the floor as the old truck lurches and rolls from side to side, ever moving forward. Rocks and gravel spew up through the hole in the floorboards, lacing the front seat with specks of mud. There is a terrible grinding crunch (at least worse than the normal terrible grinding crunches) emanating from her tortured undercarriage. She hangs up momentarily, our lives in the balance, engine screaming in protest, and then suddenly leaps forward out of the muck and bursts onto the hard gravel road beyond.

"YES!!!" The old truck careens down the hill, dropping parts hither and yon and singing now with a new and more throaty guttural roar, having changed instantaneously from a baritone to a throbbing bass. I pull over to survey the damage. Basically the muffler system is gone, the parking brake cable is dragging on the ground and there are enough rocks grinding inside the hubs to gravel a driveway. Mimi meanwhile is breathing deeply while cleaning the mud off the seats where it spewed up through the floor. The adrenalin rush is overwhelming 'cause this is Vermont living at its finest! Another magnificent spring day on Danby Mountain Road.

I once promised myself I would never write a mud season article because it had been done so many times before, but something happened this year (other than the fact I couldn't think of anything else) to change my mind. The Town of Dorset is doing some major road improvements and is actually going to fix Danby Mountain Road!! A blatant slap in the face to every good dirt-road dweller who moved to a dirt road for a reason. They're using a new technology where they put some kind of material down on the road bed and then cover it with gravel. This material prevents the water from coming up through the ground in spring thus eliminating (GASP!!) MUD SEASON!

I mean, what the hell do they think they're doing, spending my tax dollars eliminating one of Vermont's great institutions. This is tantamount to canceling deer season, banning rust on pickups or installing gas logs in the fireplace. It is these wonderful little hardships such as mud season that keep Vermont the perpetually rural state she is. If you make the living too easy, anybody can move up here. The very reason I moved up here was to experience the rural life and enjoy the adventures of living in the country. Mud season, frozen water pipes, faulty septic systems, dry wells, flooded basements, cuttin' wood, crummy TV reception, chimney fires, weekly blackouts, huntin' season, cleaning up after livestock, I mean this is livin'. Hell, it ain't no fun if everybody can do it.

It used to be the fact there was nothing to do here that kept people away, but now the advent of the information super highway (a highway which I prefer to stay the hell off) is allowing people to pursue their careers from anywhere in the world including, unfortunately, Vermont. And what makes this invasion all the more insidious is that the information superhighway don't have no mud season. Where's the adventure? Where's the challenge? Are we men or mice? Men live in parts of the country that have mud season. Mice meanwhile sit transfixed to glowing screens, basking in the electromagnetic fields that surround them, e-mailing their way through life, paying their bills by computer and group faxing each other. One of our last protections against these swarming hordes of rodent totin' Yupsters was mud season and the other wonderful inconveniences that make living here a commitment. Now, alas, technology is destroying that protection. Danby Mountain Road will become just another overpopulated road with houses stacked on top of houses, thus eliminating those other benefits of country life like walking butt naked out to the car to get something if you need to, or not having to go into the house to take a whiz if you don't want to. These are inalienable rural rights we're fighting for here.

But perhaps there is still hope. The very season of spring itself is enough to deter those of weaker constitution. We can only hope that it becomes our last line of defense. Spring is a rather paradoxical season and one must acclimate oneself over the years to become truly capable of enjoying the benefits of this remarkable season. In reality there is no more magnificent time in Vermont than when old man winter loosens his icy grip, the snow disappears in a million momentary silver rivers and the world regenerates itself once more. It is time to peel off the old shrink-to-fit plastic, remove the rotting hay bales from around the foundation, throw open the windows and doors that have been sealed for so long and once again venture out into the warmth and majesty of nature's wonder. The fact that the windows and doors are swollen shut from the moisture, the gutters are hanging down, blocking the door where the ice ripped them off the soffit, and the lawn is now a sea of formerly frozen dog crap is secondary.

Spring can be cold, warm, bright, gray, wet, dry. It is essentially meteorological schizophrenia. It is during this season that the vows of the fraternal order of resident Vermonters are renewed. It is a time when all of us must once again commit ourselves to be Vermonters through a series of rituals that involve drilling holes in trees and watching water boil, gunning our Mercedes and/or pick-ups (depending on length of Vermont tenure) through deep mud pits, totally rebuilding our houses from the destructive power of winter and most importantly exercising our democratic right to stand up at town meetings and say stuff that will cause our neighbors to hate us.

It is my intention to stand up and exercise that right to free speech and tell the town to leave my road the hell alone. If I wanted lots of neighbors and traffic I'd move to New Jersey and live on a paved road with every other mouse-clicking Tom, Dick and Harry. It's time for every good dirt-road Vermonter to stand up and protest this affront to our traditions. The only good mud season is a bad mud season. Without it, without the tales that go with it, without the exaggerations of how deep the holes were, or how terrible the damage to the car, without the commiseration and camaraderie that come with suffering through hardship together, we become just like everybody else. We lose the ability to haul each other out of the mud and make a new friend, or bring groceries to elderly neighbors whose cars can't make it down the road. Bit by bit we're chipping away at the hardscrabble soul of this rock-strewn country. Take away mud season and you take another little piece from the heart of Vermont.

Blending In: A Five-CD Set

The other evening I was standing at a cocktail party talking to two friends who, as I did, moved up here in their youth and scratched out a place for themselves. Vermont then was not a hotbed of economic opportunity and you did what was needed to survive. As hard as it was at times, it was always worth the effort. One look outside the cabin window told us that.

The advent of the information superhighway has in effect changed the dynamic of Vermont immigration. Now one simply has to move up, plug in the laptop and buy, sell or trade without missing a beat. Essentially it's Scarsdale with a better view. I worry about these people. Part of the beauty of this experience, at least for me, was in the earning. I fear these good people are missing out on the true Vermont experience. Therefore I have created a step by step course called *Blending In: A Guide for the Virgin Vermonter*. This five-CD set with accompanying hardcover manual is all you need to understand the true

Vermont experience. Just three payments of $49.95 and
I'll send you the complete set.

You'll learn all you need to know about where to
find three minimum-wage jobs—pouring liquor, hauling
wood and waiting tables—keep them all going at once,
and more importantly, where to find a place to live with a
least six other friends living on Cheetos and cheap beer.

In chapter three I'll teach you how to field strip a
chain saw, sharpen it and drop a tree next to your house
while avoiding "accidental remodeling." You'll be able
to cut, split and stack a cord of wood in an hour and not
have to add the word "amputee" to your résumé.

Want to go to that potluck supper at the firehouse? Nothing says transplant like tofu. I'll give you a complete list
of fat-laden, carbo-loaded recipes that will make you the
life of any rural potluck supper. Meat and macaroni, baby,
that's the key. Nothing like a good layer of body fat during
the Vermont winters. Wanna have some real fun? Try the
game supper. The key to blending in here is, don't ask what
you're eating. Chances are it died at the hands of a truck.

Speaking of trucks, this deluxe set will introduce you
to the joys of the rusty pickup, how to start it without
a battery and more importantly how to get it inspected
with the help of sheet metal, Bondo (a true miracle substance) and a small bribe on the side. I'll even give you a
list of dirt-road mechanics who will be glad to help you.
Nothing says Vermonter like rusty sheet metal flapping
in the wind.

One of my favorite chapters, and I'm sure it will be
yours, is mud season driving. I'll show you step by step il-
lustrations on how to negotiate the axle-sucking, exhaust-
system-shredding quagmires for which Vermont is so

famous. You'll even get to use that button on your SUV that says 4H-4L. How cool is that?

Call right now and I will include a bonus book on buying real estate in Vermont. This is an invaluable tool that will instantly clarify the mysteries of the secret Vermont real estate advertising code, such as "Vermont views" (you just bought a place in Granville, New York), or "seasonal stream" (ditch). My personal favorite is "pond site" (read: "swamp"). If they say "fixer upper, just bring a hammer," they really mean bring a hammer attached to a construction crew with some heavy equipment. Yes, folks, these little tips will make you a smart shopper for that little piece of Vermont.

One of the most popular chapters is "Building a House Under 5,000 Square Feet." Yes! It's true! You can actually live in a house smaller than the Taj Mahal and still enjoy the Vermont lifestyle. I'll show you actual pictures of Vermont houses that will fit on a 10-acre lot. Worried about living space? We'll give you tips on how to expand your horizons, like—go outside. And as an added bonus we'll teach you to landscape that house with perennials, native shrubs and a few Vermont lawn sculptures (junk cars—or even better—old tractors, a true authentic touch) and I'll show you the best galleries (okay, junkyards) to shop to make that house look like it's been here for generations.

Folks, this is a limited time offer. You don't want to miss the chapter on plumbing and how to maintain a source of water that comes from somewhere up the hill and a septic system that ends up somewhere down the hill. I'll even give you a list of plumbers that have the antiquated parts to maintain these systems and how to lure them to your house even during deer season.

One of my personal favorites is the guide to local coffee shops. This is where you can truly immerse yourself in local culture. I'll teach you how to say "small," "medium" and "large." Use the words "vente" and "grande" and you'll stick out like a Holstein in a Jersey herd and speaking of cows, you'll learn that in Vermont, soy is the main ingredient in cow feed. The only way soy gets in a cup of coffee here is by running it through a cow.

This is the chance of a lifetime and as an incentive to buy now, I'll include a pair of jumper cables, some maple syrup and a year's supply of dry gas. That's a $99 value, yours free if you call now. Just dial 555–Cow–Pies and I'll ship today.

Welcome to Vermont, folks. Living here is a privilege, simply earned by an understanding of how hard it was before it got easy. Enjoy your life here, understand it, and take care of it. If we don't, it will simply become what we left.

On Owning Land

There are some great moments in life. Those moments whose memories are never clouded by time. The birth of our children, the first car (in my case a 1959 VW convertible), sex with someone you actually like, and that moment when you become a landowner.

Whether it's a building lot in the suburbs or 500 acres in the mountains, the fact that you can stand on a piece of this earth and claim it as your own is a truly majestic feeling.

However, "owning" a piece of land is a misnomer. Long after we are dust blowing over the landscape, that particular piece of land will still exist, under the care of some other biodegradable custodian who, like ourselves, will eventually disappear. And so on.

The propinquity of man to the land is no less, if not greater than, that of man to man. If you reflect for a moment on the reason men have been killing each other over the entire course of our history, it is for the most part over this or that piece of real estate.

I myself have been custodian to a fair amount of real estate in my time. A house in the suburbs, a deer camp, a small farm, a big farm, and now six acres on a hill above Dorset. Like Goldilocks trying out the porridge and the beds, this was too small, this was too big, the one in the suburbs was too damn hot, and I'm praying this one is going to be just right. If it isn't, odds are my wife will divorce me.

Land anywhere is a living, breathing entity, with a history all its own, a personality. Like a human, land can be your friend and give you sustenance, or it can be your bitterest enemy. You can revel in your surroundings, or you can pray to God to get you the hell out of there. Each individual will exhibit a different rapport with a singular piece of land. The desert can show incomparable beauty to some, and savagely destroy others.

When building a relationship with a parcel of land, it begins to take on a character of its own. As more time is spent working the land, exploring its boundaries, it slowly reveals its secrets, both beautiful and repelling.

From the road, a breathtaking show of color from a mountain meadow can conceal the boot-sucking swamp that lies underneath the sod. On the other hand, a nondescript bunch of woods by the road can, with but a few steps into the interior, reveal a mature forest of spectacular nature.

Such was the case with the land upon which I am now building my house. When we first drove up the road the agent pointed out the markers, between which was a tangle of small roadside trees shielding any view into the land. Being at this point fairly fed up with the search, after six months of looking at this and that, I reluctantly got out of the car to "walk the land." It was early spring and the leaves had not yet formed, which made entering the lot a much simpler matter. Still unimpressed, we bushwhacked through some brambles and underbrush. I was walking with my head down, watching my step, which although important, is often the biggest mistake we can make when taking a walk in the woods.

We reached a clearing of sorts, which the realtor suggested as the best place to build the house. I finally looked up and to my surprise, a spectacular vista of mountain and valley lay stretching off to the south, through the bare trees. My halfhearted attitude dissipated. I began to pay attention, and the land began to disclose its secrets, provocatively revealing one that would then lead to another, as would an enchanting mistress.

Over the next few weeks, I made several visits to the parcel and on each occasion it divulged another segment of its character. The land had been in the same family for years and had not been logged in recent times. As we picked our way through the saplings and underbrush, we encountered huge oaks, maples and beeches, whose crowns spread high above the tangled second growth and were visible only as one came close and peered up through the lower canopy. These hidden monarchs are now beginning to reveal themselves as we clear around the building site, and push back the underbrush.

It's a bit like being a sculptor with a chainsaw. The first layers of useless material are taken away quickly, revealing a rough draft of what the finished product should be. Having removed the lower tangle, now comes the agony of picking and choosing which of the larger trees to cull in order to open and stimulate the growth of its surrounding partners. The big bucks with their imposing trunks and massive crowns are of course the heart of this sculpture and are immune to the saw, unless badly diseased and dying. It is the middle-aged trees whose destiny must be resolved. Whether they are to grow into imposing sources of shade and beauty, or provide heat for the winter, is determined by their shape, health, and proximity to other trees. In every case it is an agonizing decision and I have found myself staring at a cluster of trees trying to come to some conclusion. Once the saw enters the trunk there is no turning back. Even after I have made the choice and bury the blade into the bark there is always a second thought and hesitation. There are admittedly more than a few trees still standing that perhaps need to be removed for the health and well-being of their neighbors. Their fate, though, has been postponed in favor of an easier decision somewhere else in the woods.

To the left of the house, a stand of young birches has been thinned and opened, and now stands as a white colonnade leading toward what is, in my mind, the crowning touch to this spectacular little forest. As you leave the birch grove and head into the woods, you suddenly enter a dark, almost primeval forest of hemlocks, situated on a rock cliff. At the base of the cliff, two small streams converge in a series of small waterfalls and continue to drop over boulders and through mini-canyons as they descend down the eastern side of the property. I cannot remember in all my trips to the national forests of the Blue Ridge Mountains as a child a spot that could offer any more in the way of serenity and untouched beauty than this. That this haven resides in my backyard gives rise to a sanctimonious feeling of great wisdom that I was able to find this place, until I am humbled by the thought that I almost told the realtor to keep driving. My encounter with this small piece of heaven was the consequence of luck and a sequence of events that convince me that there is indeed a higher power watching over idiots like myself. A glance at my wife and children, and the surroundings in which we live, is irrefutable confirmation.

Index